$\mathcal{A}$ Culinary History

OF

DOWNEAST MAINE

A Culinary History

OF

DOWNEAST MAINE

SHARON L. JOYCE

AMERICAN PALATE

Published by American Palate
A Division of The History Press
Charleston, SC
www.historypress.com

First published 2019

Manufactured in the United States

ISBN 9781467138024

Library of Congress Control Number: 2019936995

Notice: The information in this book is true and complete to the best of our knowledge. It is offered without guarantee on the part of the author or The History Press. The author and The History Press disclaim all liability in connection with the use of this book.

CONTENTS

CONTENTS

To my son Jeffrey, with whom I share a lifetime pursuit of learning new things.

INTRODUCTION

The way life should be.
—Maine slogan

S o, where is Downeast Maine? Downeast Maine is usually considered the area along the coast consisting of Hancock and Washington Counties. Downeast is a nautical term meaning that if you were sailing from Boston or other southern areas in New England you would sail downwind and east to arrive on the eastern coast of Maine. Ok, it is a bit confusing. But there is another saying in Maine: "You can't get there from here." Maine is a place where roads end or begin, depending on how you look at it. Small towns, good people, some not particularly fond of those city types, various traditions and an interesting history of foods. There are treasures of natural beauty and interesting people.

You can lose yourself in thought in the natural beauty of Acadia National Park and walk along the rocky coast as you watch lobstermen haul their traps.

As you begin this book, you are probably wondering what was trending in the 1700s or if one had know at least two gelatin-based recipes in the 1950s and 1960s to be considered a good cook. What immersions and infusions were essential to Native American recipes? Perhaps you have thought about what your tastes and family background bring to what you eat. Are you influenced by foods where you live?

Maine slogan, "The way life should be." The Fourth of July parade in the Village of Bar Harbor. *Author's collection.*

Maybe you are just wondering what to have for dinner tonight or how the foods you eat affect your health.

Why is cooking too much work for some and a therapy for others? I am in neither category. I am a lifetime learner of many things. Cooking, eating, gathering together are what we build our lives around, so why not learn as much as we can about food? I have empathy for those who are overwhelmed by the number of untested recipes and food blogs that don't lead to a good final result. Hopefully, you don't give up and are happy with your mistakes. Humor is helpful.

A woman who stopped by the cooking school said she didn't cook at all. However, if she did cook, she would only be interested in "new" food cooking. She wanted to be on the cutting edge of the things she didn't do. And who is to say she wasn't? Things change, but the basics are there and, for the most part, have been there. We, as Americans, want to be the first and best, but toasting bread is toasting bread. A toaster is a toaster even though it may be bigger or a different color or faster.

I am from away. Even though I have lived in Maine for over thirty years and my son was born here, I am not considered to be from Maine. Even if you are born in Maine, you may not be considered from here by those who are from here. I do, however, have an even longer connection to Maine. When I was little, I loved lobster and would want lobster when my family went to a nice restaurant. I don't remember them ever saying that it was too expensive, even though we didn't have a lot of money. When I was in fifth grade, I had to pick a state to write a report on, and I chose Maine. I busily glued lobster shells and potato pieces on a poster and knew I had to go to Maine someday. Maine is not usually on your way somewhere else. Coming to Downeast Maine is usually a destination trip, as you are not passing through Maine to go somewhere else. So, when I had an opportunity to actually come to Maine, I took it. I stayed.

This is an understanding of the ingredients of the foods that come together in a recipe. It has been a fascinating journey for me. Why do you care about what the first inhabitants were eating or how they adapted in this new area later called Downeast Maine? It is a part of understanding yourself and opening up to creative thinking. Looking at more than a package of food at the store. It is a story about planning, organizing and stopping to think about what we eat.

1

THE FOODS THAT THE NATIVE AMERICAN "FIRST SUMMER VISITORS" FOUND ON MOUNT DESERT ISLAND

How the Ingredients Were Used and the Wisdom that Has Been Forgotten over the Years

And so it began. Many think Native Americans in Maine, as well as all indigenous people, most likely came across the Bering land bridge from Siberia to Alaska that connected the continents thirteen thousand years ago. After the ice age, there was a slow migration into various areas of the Americas, and according to the Abbe Museum in Bar Harbor, there is evidence of Native American life on Mount Desert Island over ten thousand years ago. The first to settle here were called "People of the Dawn," as those who live in this area of Maine are the first to see the sunrise in the country.

Obviously, they must have learned to look for water, certain plants and animal tracks as well as some method of catching fish during their migration. They passed down this information from generation to generation by word of mouth.

It is sometimes difficult to imagine a life without any traditional job. Their "job" in life was based on figuring out how to find food and shelter.

Corn is a good example of learning from history. Corn started in Peru, where you will find that a number of foods are thought to have originated. There is evidence of corn in the tombs of Peru as food offerings to gods and woven into fabrics and clay. It is believed that corn was cultivated by Native Americans for centuries before the European explorers arrived. The seeds and planting methods were passed on from tribe to tribe. There was wisdom in their methods of planting. Corn was sowed with a small fish for fertilizer, and beans were grown next to the newly sprouted grain so that

Acadia National Park and the views from Cadillac Mountain. *Author's collection.*

the legumes could climb the stalks. Squash was planted near the bottom of the two for shade, weed reduction and providing nitrogen to the soil. This method of planting was called Three Sisters, indicating that the three sister plants worked together to provide food for the family or tribe. Known Native American dishes like corn bread, grits, corn pudding, roasted corn and hoe and Johnny/journey cakes were part of Wabanaki culture for thousands of years. There is a wild plant in Mexico called teosinte, and it has some characteristics of modern corn. Teosinte has a hard outer shell, and when put in a fire, it pops, becoming our first form of popcorn. Pumpkin and squash were being used before the colonists arrived, and even some of these may have originated in Peru before starting their journey through America. Beans were cultivated such a long time ago it is difficult to know where their wild ancestors came from.

Beans and cornmeal keep a long time. They are easily eaten when ripe or could be dried and carried when the people seasonally migrated. They dried the corn by spreading it in the sun and keeping it away from any moisture. Then they would wrap and bury it underground for winter food. Squash and its seeds could also be dried, making perfect planting companions for this reason as well as mutual nutritional value and minimizing insect damage. Wild plants were a mainstay. Groundnuts, a type of potato-like tuber, corn, squash and beans were staples. Native Americans were clever in learning how to most successfully plant crops so that there was enough to eat and enough to store for leaner months. There was wisdom in their methods of planting

The glaciers left a rocky soil uniquely suited for Maine foods like wild blueberries and other natural foods that have been forgotten. One article said there were "tons" of edible wild plants in Maine. There are a lot of these wild plants still out there, but this is not a book on foraging.

One wild plant I use in my cooking classes is fiddlehead. This is a popular food in Downeast and grows in wet, boggy areas. It should be boiled before using to rid the fiddleheads of any toxins. After precooking, you can use it in any recipe that uses asparagus. I have even found fiddleheads in a high-end grocery store in Chicago. It is a particular fern, the Ostrich fern. They are harvested in early spring when the fern is just getting ready to open. The head, which looks like the shape of a fiddle, tastes like asparagus.

Spruce buds and tips are edible spring crops and have been used in brewing beer for centuries. In the spring, the buds from the spruce tree are harvested and eaten or dried for tea during. It has a milder taste when the

Left: Fiddleheads of the Ostrich fern are a wild indigenous food still popular in Downeast Maine today. It tastes somewhat like asparagus. *Courtesy of R.W. Buyers.*

Right: Spruce buds were eaten or used for teas and contain a high amount of vitamin C. *Author's collection.*

bud first appears. Natives gave spruce buds to sailors who were suffering from scurvy. Spruce gum was the first chewing gum in America, and it is still available. Other trees like chestnut, sassafras and certain hickory trees were used for food, medicine or strong wood to make tools. Sugar maples and yellow birch were tapped for sugar and syrup in early spring. Strawberries, raspberries and blueberries were summer harvests.

Cattails, acorns and dandelions are edible plants that people may recognize. Acorns were dried and sometimes ground and used to flavor the dried oysters, clams and mussels from an earlier season and then boiled. Many other plants grew or grow in the woods. You have to know which parts of the wild plants are edible and how to prepare and cook them or you could be sick or poisoned. Learn about them by asking a university extension agency or another reputable source. Plants were also used for medicine. The Maliseet and Passamaquoddy tell of stories passed down from ancestors who used the muskrat root as a food and medicine. Lichen could be ground for flour or used to make alcohol.

Acorns were dried and stored to be later ground into a flour. *Author's collection.*

Survival required the Wabanaki to experiment with plants, efficiently hunt, store food and find water sources. They preserved meats and used all parts of the animal. There was no waste—amazing to think of this when so much of the food we buy today is thrown away in landfills.

Corn is an example of what the Wabanaki did with leftover remnants of their food. Think about this when you go to the store. The corn would usually be boiled and eaten or used in making soup. Portions of the corn harvest would be dried and saved for later use. The outer husks would be saved for cooking foods in them, making mats and baskets, clothing or dolls for children to play. The silk would be cooked for a tea or broth and was also dried and used in the other seasons. It has a mild taste. The cob would be dried and used as a fire starter. No trash here.

Learning to improvise is a good trait for anyone, but Native Americans had to adapt to their food resources. They understood their foods with a wisdom that has been lost to most people. Today, we get food from all regions of the world, and in many cases, we don't know what additives have infiltrated into the foods we eat.

There was an abundance of foods in Maine, particularly along the coast. These hunter-gatherers moved at different times of the year to take advantage of the plentiful seasonal foods, fish runs and animal migration. Wabanaki learned to eat, process and store what was available during different seasons. They needed tools to produce foods and build homes. Rakes, hoes and digging tools made from stone, bones, antlers, shells and wood were used. Wabanaki studied their foods and nature. Hunting for forest animals and fishing were the primary sources for protein, and their diets were then completed with seasonal fruits and vegetables. There was a thoughtful appreciation of all foods that the gods provided them. They didn't kill just for sport; they used every part of the animal, and many felt that every creature was sacred. They embraced the joy and festivity of gathering wild berries and other food sources. Entertainment was centered on the food and festivity of the harvest of each season. Wild plants were used for cooking, medicine and worshipping the gods.

The Wabanaki tribes had thirteen months on their calendar. Migration from the inland areas during the winter to the coast during warmer months allowed the people to take advantage of winter hunting and the coastal abundance of fish and berries.

Strawberries were harvested when the smaller strawberry moon appeared. They celebrated with a drink consisting of a strawberry-flavored water with a little maple syrup for sweetening. A hard cookie/cracker for

Raspberries were a seasonal food eaten at the time of picking or dried for later use in foods such as stews. *Author's collection*.

Fields of fresh wild blueberries. *Author's collection*.

travel or for longer "shelf life" was made from water and strawberries mashed and added to cornmeal with a little maple syrup and baked. Strawberries were the first crop to begin the growing season.

Blueberries were considered a gift from the gods. The end of the fruit has the appearance of five points of a star. It was said to have been created by the Great Spirit to feed Indian children during a famine. The plant grows larger each year, and with its spreading rhizomes, a single blueberry plant could possibly grow to the size of a football field. The blueberry had a number of other uses such as a medicine for coughs or other illnesses, dried provisions for long travels and dye for baskets.

Cattail was not only prized for basket and mat making: many parts of the plant are edible, including the roots, young shoots, stalks and even the pollen, which is rich in amino acids and protein. A good source of carbohydrates, traditionally, the roots and stalks of the cattail are prepared by baking them in ashes.

Deer, moose, rabbit, beaver, muskrat, gulls, bear, caribou, birds such as grouse and other animals were killed and roasted, smoked, boiled in a stew or dried in very thin strips near a fire or in the sun. Meat preserved by smoking was an important part of the Wabanaki diet. The meat would be

Cattails were a source of food for the Wabanaki, and a flour was made from the pollen. *Author's collection.*

cut in small strips and hung next to the fire until it was dry like leather. Boiling meat was done in hollowed-out logs or birchbark pots. Rocks would be heated and added to the food pot for cooking. Bird eggs such as gull were valued. Meat was added to other ingredients to make a stew. Any animal could make up the next meal in hard times. They hunted with dogs, and most hunters had their own dogs. The dogs were fed with the parts of the animal that couldn't be used for their normal cooking. Meat was cooked and not eaten raw. Also, Wabanakis did not generally eat snakes or frogs except when starving. Turtles were boiled and cut in pieces for a stew.

Wabanaki legend shows Gooskup/Glooskabe/Glooskap/Glooscap as a mystical, magical, mischievous and virtuous figure who was the teacher and guide of the Wabanaki people. There are a number of spellings of the name depending on the tribe. The Abbe Museum in Bar Harbor, Maine, uses the spelling Glooscap. Glooscap used stories and humor to teach his people right and wrong and instilled human values. There are a number of Wabanaki stories that are fun to read and thought-provoking. The Abbe Museum in Bar Harbor has more information about these legends. The general feeling of the Abernaki Glooskabe legend of maple syrup is that there is more of an appreciation for what you have if you have to work for it. Glooskabe arrived at his people's village and heard the moaning of his people in the forest. When he got to the area, he found his people not in pain but moaning in enjoyment from drinking the syrup as it flowed from the maple tree. They were lying around drinking the freely flowing nectar from a branch that was pulled off. Glooskabe told his people to return to work, but they didn't want to, as they were enjoying the syrup. He wanted them to understand the value of working for what you want. He poured water into the tree, making the maple tree so that you had to collect the watery liquid and then boil it for hours to get the final syrup to enjoy and this was only possible once a year. This story was passed down through many generations, and the story varies with years of retelling this valuable lesson. This and many other legends may be found online at native-languages.org.

Many meals were flavored with animal fats. The fat of animals like bear, porpoise, seal and raccoon were used for skin protection from heat or cold and for cooking. Later, the fats would also be helpful in trade with explorers to use in watches and oil lamps and on door hinges.

The ocean was rich with sea life. The Wabanakis found clams and oysters in the mudflats, and mussels were plentiful on nearby tidal rocks. Mussels attach themselves to the rocky coast in one spot and stay in that same place their entire lives. Clams were the most plentiful. Bar Harbor's name translates to "clam gathering place." They were roasted or perhaps boiled in birchbark baskets or hollowed-out logs. Shells attached to wood would be used for tools and for cooking. Rocks would be added to the fire or in or on pots for cooking. Many shell heaps are found from the remains of the Wabanaki feasts on Mount Desert Island and along the Downeast coast.

Excavations along the coast brought about an interesting study of the Native diet. David Sanger at the University of Maine found, "Strangely, Native inhabitants seem to have avoided lobsters; we have found only one claw in twenty years of excavation in coastal Maine sites." They did find some bones from fish, seal and porpoise. Seal and porpoise had highly valued oil used for cooking, and their skins were cured for clothing and shelter.

There were many fish, such as flounder, haddock, salmon, trout and smelt. Cod and mackerel were caught farther out in the ocean by nets. Those fish closer in could be caught by making a weir and then using the natural tide rhythm to trap the fish. A weir is a number of twigs that make a semicircle fence-like trap. The fish would then be caught in a woven bag or by using spears. They would come in to feed at high tide, and when the tide changed, the door to the weir would be pushed closed by the outgoing tide. Occasionally, a whale would be grounded and would be a major production by many with spears or harpoons.

Fish were usually roasted, dried or smoked on a plank over an open fire. The backbones of eels were used in corn soup. The fall meant drying and salting fish for winter survival. This was sometimes done by taking off the head, cleaning the fish and then nailing it up against a wooden structure to dry in the sun.

Wabanaki seasonal migration was like going to a grocery store and shopping mall. There was excitement when they found food that also gave them clothes, body lotions, fashion ornaments, cooking utensils, hooks, needles, pots and medicine.

Breads were made from various ingredients but especially corn. A hoe cake was the simplest form and still tastes good today. Foods were either roasted, boiled or salted. Simple soups were made of what you had and seasonal variety.

Strawberry-flavored water was special during the strawberry season in the 1600s, and flavored water is here today. They would add the mashed strawberry to water. This beverage was particularly used during the strawberry moon and festival celebrating the strawberry season and thanking the gods for this gift. Soups were possible in 1600s using any the ingredients that they would find seasonally such as minced onion cooked in fats, corn broth made from corn silk and / or vegetable broth, any vegetables in season were possible soups. A type of tuber called *hopniss* (potato) was available at times, as was fish or meat. Roasted squash over a fire could be combined with any berries or corn stuffing. Spruce buds could also be made into a tea or broth for a soup base.

The early explorers needed to find goods and produce that would be valuable to the Native Americans for trade. As the Wabanaki migrated seasonally, lightweight metal pots that could be easily transported were popular items, and the Natives also appreciated new crops, such as peas, that Europeans introduced to the North American continent.

———•———

RECIPES

Pemmican

Wabanaki would have used deer, elk, moose or other dried meat, as cattle had not yet been imported by the colonies. The meat would be lean, with the fat kept to use for cooking. The fruit used was seasonal or dried. Wabanaki knowledge of food preparation enabled the resources to last a long time, and this process for drying food is still used.

Very thoroughly dried beef
Hot fat
Chopped dried fruit

Finely grind dried meat into a powder. Heat fat until very hot and add to beef enough that it holds together. Add fruit, which would have been optional. Place in a shallow pan, and as it cools, cut in bars or smaller portable shapes.

Hoe Cake

1 cup cornmeal
Water

Add boiling water until the cornmeal is the consistency of a pourable batter. Let it rest for five minutes and add a little more water if needed. Place a little oil on a heavy pan and cook the batter on fairly high heat on one side before flipping it over. Cornmeal was easily transported, and only water was needed to cook on a hoe over an open fire.

A basic bread for breakfast, lunch or dinner.

2

THE EFFECTS OF DIFFERENT CULTURES AND HERITAGE ON DOWNEAST FOOD

Are you sitting and enjoying your spruce tip tea? Note that if you were to actually make this tea, you should know that if the tips are cut in early spring, they have a slight lemony flavor. Spruce is loaded with vitamins C and A and has antimicrobial and antibacterial properties.

There was a great deal of exploration by the English, French and others for trade and then land for colonization. Explorers' view of Indians and reports back to their countries differed. In the sixteenth century, the Spanish were told of gold mines by the Natives. Natives were referred by Spanish explorers as people "from beyond the bounds of Christendom who had never been baptized" and "naked slaves of the Devil," as one annalist described them. Later, the British and French found that the Native Americans were a healthy and attractive people with an understanding of the land. Cultural differences, attitudes and communication would bring continual problems.

Next is the story of peas. Yes, peas. The account of the popular English pea follows. Throughout history, people have learned from James Rosier's written account of the 1605 Weymouth voyage. In 1605, the English captain George Weymouth made a voyage to the Maine coast and kidnapped five Native Americans. There is some question of exactly where the kidnapping took place. Some think that it was in the Penobscot Bay in Downeast, and others believe that it was farther south. Word spread from tribe to tribe and across the country. The Wabanaki Federation was created in 1606 for the safety of the people and their lands. It comprised the Wabanaki, Micmac, Penobscot, Maliseet and Passamaquoddy tribes.

As Captain Weymouth explored the coast of Maine in 1605, he kidnapped five Natives with the lure of a can (cup) of pease (peas). In order to make friends and barter for goods, food was usually offered to the Indians. Three came aboard ship with the promise of more peas below deck, and then they were locked in. Several more were then forcibly taken from the shore. Word spread between tribes that the families were near the shore pleading for the return of their loved ones. Rosier's account of Weymouth's voyage said that it was the plan to capture Natives and then teach them the English language and use them for guides. Eventually, several Wabanaki were returned years later, and there were reports that one died as a slave in Spain.

In Weymouth's ship account of the kidnapping, please note that canning as we know it was not invented at that time. The dried peas were probably made into a type of soup in a cup, not a can as we think of a can today. The explorers even wrote that the Natives were polite and returned the cans in which food was taken from the ship and given to their families. Peas were very popular in England at the time, and dried peas traveled well and were good for food on board and for trade.

There are other accounts of that voyage that give an indication of what foods the voyage suggested could be potentially grown in this new area. It would have been foods that would have appealed to the British and what England was eating at that time. In 1605, Weymouth planted a garden containing peas, barley and garden seeds—an incentive for people interested in starting colonies.

The ship's journal indicates that the explorers found "plenty of salmon and other fishes of great bigness; good lobsters, rock fish, plaice and lumps…and with two or three hooks caught about 30 great cod and haddock, to supply the ship's company for three day; and the shores, abundance of great mussels, some of which contained pearls; fourteen taken from a single one." They also found currants, spruce, yew, angelica, various trees and other plants.

The foods found onshore were a pleasant surprise for explorers, as the food carried onboard usually included salt pork, ship's biscuit made of flour and water and rum to drink. From 1677 to 1740, the British Royal Navy rations per man per day were "One pound biscuit, 1 gallon of beer, four pounds of beef, two pounds of salt pork, 3/8 of a 24 inch cod, two pints of peas, six ounces of butter, and eight to twelve ounces of cheese." Later, in 1731, the Royal Navy replaced the fish with three pints of oatmeal. If the sailors ever got fresh bread, they would reuse the leftovers and bake it again as rusk.

French explorer Samuel de Champlain also explored the Downeast in 1605. Champlain spoke of planting Brazil beans (today's equivalent of lima beans) in Maine during a voyage.

He traded biscuits, tobacco and other trifles to the Wabanaki for fish and beaver. These plantings by the English and French would later determine the potential profits for their countries and for convincing people to come to America with the expectation of cultivating the same crops from home for comfort and survival.

Cultural differences started miscommunication problems from the beginning, particularly regarding how the new explorers and Indians felt about one another and their food. The Natives were noted by early explorers to be attractive healthy people with a balanced diet of plants, animals and fish. There was no disease, and there were no signs of those with physical or mental ailment. Of course, that changed with the European diseases that were to follow as settlements were established. These European diseases included measles, smallpox and the common cold. Native Americans had no immunity for these new diseases, and as a result, thousands died along the Downeast coast.

One of the biggest problems for explorers back then was the limited amount and variety of foods that traveled well. Fruit was perishable, so sailors had a high level of mortality due to scurvy. The Natives cured many of the sailors who had scurvy with spruce tips or buds. Spruce tips and buds were dried and available as a tea, eaten right off the new tip of a branch or prepared in recipes. Spruce tips have a very high concentration of vitamin C and are sometimes still used in beer production even today.

Unfortunately, it was only a week after Weymouth had captured the Natives when Champlain sailed the Maine coast and was met with some distrust. Some stories of the kidnapping relate that the English killed the five captured. The Natives were aware that the English felt they were superior, and the colonists made it known that the English owned the land now. The English didn't appreciate or understand Native American worship, their homes, their clothes and their seasonal migration—or their food. The French appeared to appreciate the cultural differences, and they learned from the Wabanaki people. The French didn't push the fact that they too "owned" the land but explained they were there in an advisory role. And the French didn't try to capture Natives with the lure of "pease."

When John Smith made an observation of Mount Desert Island on his voyage of 1614, he noted that there were "as many clams and lobsters as you would like." It was easy for explorers to stock up on food to continue their voyage.

What did the Wabanaki think of the explorers? In 1606, the Wabanaki tribe federation was formed to protect their rights and their land.

Remember that the Wabanaki didn't have the brick-and-mortar homes that the Europeans were used to. They migrated by seasons. The Europeans thought no one lived in certain areas because they saw no permanent structures. So, they set up their homes in areas that were actually inhabited by Indian tribes. This was a problem. The Wabanaki returned when it was time to harvest or hunt to find that Europeans had moved in. Colonists were on important Native grounds that provided people food. The cultures clashed, as each thought the other should be more like them. Worship was a big part of the culture of the Wabanaki people, and they worshiped the gods that gave them their food. The gods taught them values and to appreciate all nature. Europeans thought the Indians were savages and that they should become Christians. The Wabanaki were very well adapted to their surroundings. If someone in the tribe didn't have enough to eat, they would be given food by the others. Europeans did not want to change their habits but really needed the Wabanaki for survival.

Colonies were formed, and Native Americans taught their planting practices to the settlers. The Native methods out-produced English methods of planting. The Wabanaki were survivors and did their best not to be dominated by the white settlers, who continually took more and more of their land and way of life. Many conflicts occurred. At one point, the English demanded full loyalty from the Native Americans. The Wabanaki did not want to fight against the French, so they explained to the English that the French were their brothers and the English their cousins. After the Seven Years' War, the English were now the rulers of this land and the boundaries of Indian land kept getting more restrictive. Their areas for hunting, fishing and planting became smaller and smaller.

The Europeans wanted trade of valuable fur, animal skins, feathers, baskets and plants like sassafras, which was used as a medicine in Europe. The Wabanaki traded for farming tools, hunting weapons, pots/kettles and other cooking utensils. Knowledge of food was shared.

Colonies started to take hold, and permanent settlements were established. More and more of the products and comforts of home were brought over from Europe, and other customs trickled down into Downeast Maine. The English were building their stone-and-brick structures. Wheat, cows, pigs and chickens were brought over from England, and homes were built. Trade increased, and some spices, molasses and rum showed up.

The new foods meant that more of a variety of recipes could be produced. Indian Pudding, brown bread, salt pork, ham, beef, succotash, English-style biscuits, cakes and fruit pies were now possible for English colonists. In the 1600s, many colonists ate from wooden bowls and had few utensils, but English china was soon to follow. Slowly, these pieces of personal property became symbols of stature and wealth.

Water was the method of travel, and Maine had many waterways, including the Penobscot River, which would become a major transportation route for lumber as well as other goods from Bangor to Downeast Maine and beyond. Sea trade was the colonists' goal, and industry was just beginning in Downeast, showing the way to wealth in the New World. The sea provided food and transported food. Keeping foods from spoiling was done without the use of refrigeration or canning, As it had for thousands of years, preservation was done by drying and salting the food to rid it of moisture. Today, companies use drying to sell spices, and at home, people dry foods with dehydrators. In Downeast, the fresh fish would be gutted and heads cut off. The fish would then be laid out in the sun to dry. Fish flakes, as they are called, would be all along the coast where fishermen brought in fish. In Eastport, there were Herrin Horses where fishermen would hang herring that were too big to can as sardines, and they would smoke them over a fire.

Ships needed to be built, and the New World's first big shipbuilding industry started in Maine. The lumber industry started on the coast and moved inland as the colonists cut down most of the saleable trees. Maine had white pine trees. They grow tall and straight and are perfect for a ship's mast. Besides fur trade, a great fortune could be made from wood, which was highly depleted in Europe. Much of the lumbering was done in the winter when it was easier to move logs in snow. In the spring, they would float the logs downriver. Europeans started hearing of the great opportunities in the New World. The British had forced the French from Nova Scotia, and British and Scotch-Irish began settling in Downeast Maine. This was important for drawing workers for the lumber industry. You needed water to move the logs, and you needed food to feed the new arrivals working in the lumber industry. As the lumber became scarce, the waterways of inland Maine became even more important in getting lumber to the sea and to boat-building companies along the coast.

In the lumber camps, the cook was very important and could threaten to leave if he was not treated well. With a bad cook or no cook, the lumbermen would have a difficult time surviving. Lumbering was hard and dangerous

Fish flakes were a method of drying fish on racks. Higgins Wharf, Bernard, Maine. *Courtesy of the Southwest Harbor Library*.

work. The cook needed to be able to be creative in using a limited number of ingredients in many ways. That was the sign of a good cook. What ingredients did they usually have to work with in a lumber camp? Flour, salted meats, salted fish, some type of fat, beans, molasses, gingerbread, potatoes and blocks of tea that the cook would cut off a piece to use to boil the tea. Coffee wasn't popular at the time and was also too heavy to transport in comparison to blocks of tea. You needed things that were as easy to carry as possible or that were available when you got where you were going. Since lumbermen couldn't rely on finding food when they arrived at their camp, they needed to be well supplied and flexible and plan ahead. Sometimes, pickerel—a fish available year-round—would be caught. They live in weeded shallow water and were caught by spear usually. Animals might be in the area where lumbermen were harvesting wood but couldn't be counted on. After canning was invented, the possibilities increased, but that was much later.

Have you ever been camping with the understanding that a grocery store would not be an option? What if you didn't plan well? What would we learn from that type of experience in planning foods at home? Using up all your food would prevent food waste and save money.

So, everyone was happy, right? Well, not really. In 1729, the English marked a huge amount of trees to reserve them for themselves. The English continued to add taxes on items like molasses. This didn't make the colonists happy. The Wabanaki were losing their hunting grounds (and their spruce buds), and the sawdust from the sawmills was polluting the waters. But someone was making money, and the food on their dinner tables was a bit more elaborate. Wealth was made, but nature wasn't doing too well.

The English colonists wanted the foods from home because they felt English food was superior and gave the comfortable feeling of home in this new world. In general, they didn't want the food that the Wabanaki people ate. They wanted what the king of England was eating.

The English preferred wheat over corn, and with the milk from cows brought here and eggs from English chickens, they were now able to make all the baked goods that reminded them of home. Sweeteners like honey, maple syrup and molasses were readily available. Meat from imported farm animals like cattle and pigs was starting to replace game animals. The English brought seeds like flowers and vegetables and planted herbs in their gardens for medicinal reasons and for the feeling of home. The Irish, Scots and French had moved into Nova Scotia and then migrated into what is now northern Maine and Washington County. They brought their comfort foods like *ploys* and *fin and hattie*.

Groundnuts/hopniss were the wild tubers (early potatoes) first widely used in Downeast Maine by indigenous people. The potato that we recognize today has an interesting history. The Spanish took the potato from Mexico to Spain in 1520 and then brought it to Florida in 1560. An Irish genealogist at a talk in Chicago's Newbury Library assured the audience that the potato came to the United Kingdom from a colony in Virginia by Sir Walter Raleigh in 1589 and it was first planted at Sir Walter Riley's estate in Ireland. The English captain took it to Ireland, and the Irish-type potato was then brought to Maine. There was a misconception in the very early days that potatoes caused diseases like leprosy and fevers. This false information took some time for people to forget. French King Louis XVI eating potatoes comforted people. He wore potato blossoms in his lapel and served potatoes at his table. One story goes that this Irish-type potato was introduced by the French into Maine. The other story says that Irish workers started planting the potato here in the 1700s. The potato had become popular in Ireland by 1771. And now it was here.

———•———

Recipes

Wilted Dandelions

1 egg, slightly beaten
½ cup cream
1 tablespoon butter
2 tablespoons apple cider vinegar
Salt and pepper
Fresh dandelion greens

Stir all ingredients but greens in a saucepan until the mixture thickens. Pick dandelion greens before they flower. Tear leaves into small pieces and add to heated mixture.

• • •

Hasty Pudding

Corn had been a basic food in the colonial household since the Indians had taught the early settlers how to grow corn and grind it into cornmeal. Hasty pudding is a cornmeal mush, easy to make and nutritious. It became a popular food, as did journey/Johnny cakes.

2½ cups water
¾ teaspoon salt
1 cup cornmeal

Boil the water and salt. Sprinkle cornmeal over water, stirring constantly. Simmer for 30 minutes, stirring occasionally. Serve like oatmeal with milk, molasses, maple syrup, honey or sugar.

• • •

Fried Hasty Pudding

Pour the hasty pudding into a loaf pan and let it cool in the refrigerator until firm. Cut into ¾-inch slices and fry in sunflower oil until brown and crusty on both sides. Serve with maple syrup or molasses. In today's cooking, use organic sunflower oil, as it is a high-heat oil and has no taste. Blend molasses with butter to make a molasses butter topping.

• • •

Journey Cake, or Johnny Cake

This cake has similar ingredients to hoe cake and was made even more popular with the addition of milk, after cows were brought from England.

2 cups cornmeal
1 teaspoon salt
Hot water
Milk
Butter

Add cornmeal and salt to scalding water, stir until thick and then thin with milk. Cook in a heavy pan with a little butter. A sweetened Johnny cake was another variation a cook could make:

Boiling water
7 tablespoons cornmeal
1 tablespoon sugar
½ teaspoon salt
½ cup milk
Butter

Pour boiling water over next three ingredients—just enough water to make a batter—then thin with milk. Cook with a little butter in a pan.

• • •

Indian Cakes

This recipe has a light cornbread taste and is from the Bangor Historical Society reproduction of the book The Sanitary Fair Cook Book, Bangor, *1864.*

1 tablespoon butter
1 cup cornmeal
1 cup flour
¼ cup sugar
1 teaspoon cream of tartar
½ teaspoon baking soda
1 egg
1 cup milk

Preheat oven to 350 degrees. While oven is preheating, put butter in a round cake pan or, preferably, cast-iron pan in oven to melt butter. Sift together dry ingredients. Beat eggs and milk together. Mix with dry ingredients, stirring just until combined. Pour batter into prepared pan. Bake 25 minutes, until lightly browned. Makes 8 servings.

———◆———

In late nineteenth-century cookbooks, you will see several types of recipes that were an indication of the times by using newer available ingredients like wider usage of milk and butter.

Colonial hoe cakes were basically cornmeal and water as discussed earlier and just called hoe cakes. Now that changes were made with the addition of milk and butter, they needed to be called something different to distinguish between the old and new.

3

WATERPOWER AND INDUSTRY CREATE A GROWING POPULATION WITH INCREASES IN THE DEMAND FOR FOOD

The early settlers established permanent fishing stations, and until the mid-1700s, fishing was the primary industry. But other industries were in place to overtake the fishing industry in revenue and increase the possibilities for wealth.

The late 1700s enabled Maine to get a number of new food influences due to inhabitants coming to Downeast Maine because of disaster and wars. The Maine Wabanaki were forced north to Canada or into Downeast Maine during the French and Indian War. In 1755, the Acadians were forced out of Nova Scotia to Maine, and in 1847, the potato famine brought Maine an increased Irish population along with crops of Irish potatoes. Some settlers stayed in Downeast, and some eventually moved elsewhere. They left their mark on the foods of Downeast.

The 1765 Quartering Act made a provision that British soldiers were to be given food and shelter at the colonists' expense. The British could place troops in an individual's home for room and board for free when they wanted to and needed no permission from the homeowner. Having a British soldier staying in your house meant having to be very careful about what you said. Colonists were not happy that the British felt they had the authority to place soldiers in their homes. This resentment could have been shown in the foods they cooked or the names they gave the foods publicly or privately. A possible resentment against the British rule showed in one way by the early colonists adding blueberries to traditional English puddings and cakes and calling them by new names like grunt, buckle and slump.

But there also are characteristics of the cooking of these dishes that could explain the names officially created in the 1800s. Take a look at these dishes to see the traditional differences. Crumbles and crisps are basically the same, but sometimes crisps don't contain oatmeal. The topping of a crisp might be of flour, nuts, sugar, butter, graham cracker or cookie crumbs and bread crumbs. A cobbler is usually fruit again but topped with a drop-type biscuit so it resembles a cobblestone street. A buckle places a cake-like mixture under the fruit, and it rises through the fruit during baking. Grunts are cooked on top of the stove, and as the fruit cooks the dumpling gets steamed; the slump is also cooked on top of the stove.

Too many taxes. England now had control and began to make more money by taxing many of the products that were available like sugar, molasses and tea. Restrictive living conditions built resentment in the colonies along with the molasses tax, sugar tax, marking and keeping the good trees and then tea. After the Boston Tea Party, Americans began thinking coffee should be their morning drink, and its popularity has expanded ever since. Tea did have certain advantages, though. Tea was sold in blocks and was lighter to transport by horse and carriage.

The Revolutionary War brought about a significant change in food availability and preparation. The import of cattle made meat supplies possible during a time when there was a scarcity of meat People started raising more cattle for sale. Butter was used more. In Downeast, salt pork was still the staple fat, and the major use was for making dinners. Butter use was growing faster than the other fats. It was becoming more available, and people did not have to have a storage of bear fat or other animal fats. Also, the French were on the Americans' side in this conflict, so more French foods were accepted. With that came butter and sauces. In Downeast, people started drinking more coffee.

The Wabanaki sided with the colonists. The Machias residents in Downeast Maine captured the first British ship of the Revolutionary War in 1775.

On July 4, 1776, it was time to celebrate. So, everyone sat down to a lobster dinner? No, actually people ate according to what was available seasonally. In the 1700s, celebrations were formed around food and foods that were available. President John Adams celebrated the Fourth of July in 1776 with poached salmon, new peas, new potatoes and strawberry shortcake. Why? The salmon had started running, the new potatoes and peas were harvested and strawberries were ripe and available. Much of that meal became a tradition in Downeast Maine for a long time. Of course, the lobster and corn often appear in the feast on the Fourth of July in present times. Salmon or strawberries were special because you only had a period of time to enjoy this seasonal food before you would have to wait for a year. It was a different way of thinking.

European fishing interests had slowed down. Water power was the resource that was crucial to the promise that Maine would become the leading industrial state. Lumbering started along the coast and then went inland and near rivers to bring the wood to where it could be floated downstream. Goods needed to go down the Penobscot River to the ocean before being shipped to Europe or major cities along the Atlantic coast. Water power created many possibilities; the textile industry used our abundance of water power and flourished. Wood was loaded on ships being built in Downeast. Stone and brick were needed to build factories, and entire communities were established to house workers for quarries in Downeast Maine. They all needed to eat. Sardine factories in Downeast were established, providing jobs and food. Fishing and raising animals for slaughter increased. Ice was harvested for food preservation and shipped to all regions and large cities. Family farms were an important part of living. Wild blueberries were harvested. Homes were built using Maine lumber and painted using paint made from blueberries boiled in milk. Industry was on the rise.

Downeast Maine had what many states didn't have and that was abundant water power. People bought land and moved from other areas to take advantage of the beautiful area, abundant food and moneymaking opportunities. Harbors were busy. Industry was growing, and people, including the Wabanaki, found seasonal jobs. Harvesting food during the summer, raking blueberries in August, digging potatoes in fall, lumbering in winter, harvesting maple syrup in March and driving logs down rivers in the spring were all possibilities.

Many people saw the opportunities for wealth. Sometimes, learning is turning off the main road. Columbia Falls has the Ruggles House Historical Home Museum. Thomas Ruggles settled there at the end of the eighteenth century and built a formidable home between 1818 and 1820. Columbia Falls became an active town with a hotel, tavern, restaurant and store. Today, the commercial aspect of the town has disappeared. Ruggles bought plantation no. 13 in a place that would become the state of Maine a few years later. He took advantage of the financial gains in harvesting lumber and in the shipbuilding business and made a lot of money. His land had thousands of wooded acres, and he built his own ships to transport the wood. The family had vegetable, fruit and herb gardens and farm animals. With wealth

Mary Chandler was the first woman pharmacist in Maine. *Courtesy of the Ruggles House Historical Home Museum.*

comes status and a better home than anyone else. He also had all the titles that a small area could give you. He died later the same year the house was completed. There is a certain wry sense of humor in Downeast, Maine. His epitaph reads, "In human hearts what bolder thought can rise / Than man's presumption on tomorrow's dawn."

His granddaughter's cousin Mary Chandler was the first woman pharmacist in Maine and would gather herbs from her garden for remedies. Plants like dandelions, anise, parsley and witch hazel were planted, grown and harvested. The apothecary shop was next door to the Ruggles House. Mary Chandler brought the Ruggles House when it was in bad repair and had it restored. The Ruggles family had farm animals for food. In the backyard, workmen found numerous animal bones during excavation. Dandelions have always been a delight to children as they bend the stem over and shoot the flower or make a wish and send hundreds of seeds into the air.

Maine has always used its natural resources. Wood, granite, slate and brick made Maine a contributor not only to the nation's housing but also to historic buildings, roads and American infrastructure. Hall Quarry on Mount Desert Island is a quiet residential area. It used to be a bustling town of around five thousand inhabitants. Granite was shipped all over the country. The stone industry attracted many foreign workers, including talented stone carvers from Italy. The Italians lived in Hall Quarry in an area referred to as "macaroni hill." Italians referred to any pasta as macaroni. Macaroni also was a slang for a dandy. Remember the song "Yankee Doodle Dandy"? "Put a feather in his hat and called it macaroni." Pasta was added to soups and the traditional Italian foods that were from their homeland of Italy. According to *The History of Maine*, there was a continuing demand for granite, and in 1875, Maine shipped four and a half million tons to areas to build buildings, bridges and roads. The curator at the Maine Granite Museum on Mount Desert Island said that sometimes granite and ice would be shipped together.

Sardines were processed in along the coast of Downeast after the process of canning was introduced into America in New York in 1812 by Robert Ayars. Canning had been invented in France when Napoleon held a contest to make it easier for his troops to transport and have ample

Dandelion plant was imported from England because of nutritional and medicinal properties All parts of the flower may be eaten. *Author's collection.*

food as they moved around. Nicholas Apart won the contest and started the first canning manufacturing plant in France. This idea was improved on in 1810, and the tin can was patented by English merchant Nicholas Durant. By the time of the Civil War, commercial canning had begun in America. This became very important in the growth of Downeast Maine products. Foods were transported to the troops. Sardines were being canned, but demand for canned sardines was slow, so the sardine cannery used containers for canning wild blueberries. This was the beginning of the widespread popularity of the Downeast wild blueberry.

Tastes changed, and the popularity of cod declined in the mid-1800s, and smoked fish like mackerel and herring became the popular trending seafood. In 1873, canning fish expanded the Maine fish market. Large schools of sardines were harvested. Herring that were too large for canning were hung on a Herrin Horse for smoking. Commercial lobster fishing began in the 1800s, and sardines were also an important bait to attract lobsters into traps and still are.

What foods did people yearn for? The Newberry Library in Chicago has letters that a soldier wrote home to his aunt living in New England during the Civil War. Edward Curtis's handwritten letters are dated between 1855 and 1865 and were sent to his aunt while he was stationed in Tennessee. On February 12, 1863, Curtis requested that his aunt send him "recipe for biscuits as you make them." He also asked how to make a good corn cake and a pie crust. On March 27, 1863, Edward Curtis sent his aunt some prickly pear seeds and reported that he made a few biscuits in a Dutch oven with a few coals on top. He said they were "good as he expected but baked a little too fast." On August 10, 1863, Curtis wrote that they had gotten rations of five fall apples, corn, peaches and apples that were not quite ripe. He said he baked a pie the day before and "biscuits today with pretty good success." "I have pancakes often, as good as the best minus butter to eat with them." He also spoke of blackberries he picked near their camp close to Murfreesboro, Tennessee, and said there weren't many fruit trees except peach trees. He asked for things that he missed being away from home.

At the Bar Harbor Historical Society, there is an 1865 diary of Daniel S. Chase from East Machias, who served in the Civil War in Virginia and fought in Gettysburg. His diary lists his food during the winter and then a quick change to his farming activity back at home in Maine after the war ended. There are clues as to what foods were available. The food that he purchased included apples, milk, cheese, crackers, potatoes, bread, cake, pie, candy, sugar, beef, molasses and beer. Did he grow the rest? Among the items he bought were fish hooks. Several diary entries follow:

January 21, 1865

We had for breakfast beans, bread and butter and coffee. It commenced to rain in the morning about four o'clock and froze as it came rained all day, a cold storm not able to work excused. Did not eat any supper, Wind NE

Sunday January 22, 1865

For breakfast bread and butter and coffee. Dull weather all day. Wind NE. Sick Did not eat any dinner. For supper dried apples bread and butter, coffee, fresh beef. Did not eat much

February 6, 1865

No breakfast doctor came to visit, dinner bred and beef, supper bread, molasses and tea. Having a battle today on the Southside railroad or Hatches run.

February 8, 1865

Battle still breakfast bread and pork, dinner been soup 12 car loads of wounded.

Sunday February 12, 1865

Breakfast bread and coffee, dinner fresh beef, potatoes bread and tea supper bread meat tea at the tent.

February 20,1865

Bought hard cheese and sugar at comasary [sic]

In March 1865, other items like pickled pigs' feet, fish, potatoes, oyster stew and onions were mentioned for breakfast. On April 12, 1865, Chase said they marched, and on the way, a Mr. Estes gave them corn bread and ham. On April 19, 1865, he reported that Lincoln was killed and an "armistus" agreed upon for ten days. In May 1865, Daniel Chase may have returned home, as he stopped talking about what he was eating and said he was "cutting potatoes to plant…Planted squash and split wood":

June 10, 1865

Planted cucumbers

August 5, 1865

Saturday went to town got meal corn and fish

September 8, 1865

Mowed oats today

September 9, 1865

Spread out oats hauled in oats in afternoon

September 15, 1865

Thrashing oats, pulling peas in forenoon

September 19, 1865

Digging up potatoes dug six bushels went to town got 1 pound tea paid 1.25

For the rest of September and November 1865, he worked in the sawmill and talked about snow in late November. On December 16, Chase "killed [a] hog in the forenoon. Cut the hog up in the afternoon the hogs wate [*sic*] was 270 pounds." At the end of the diary were several partial recipes. This is one of them:

Dreid apple pie. Stew the apple mash them up sweeten them put in butter, salt and spice crust, take a larg_ of lard or butter to a quart of flour rub the lard into the dry flour first and then take water enough to mix it take a little roll it out quite thin and put it on the plate trim it off.

After the Civil War, Maine's canning business grew. In *History of Maine*, author Williamson includes state manufacturing statistics for 1873: "From a small beginning, the packing business in Maine has assumed enormous proportions. It is universally conceded that the best canned corn comes from Maine, and that the largest lobster factories are located in this State."

It went on to say that corn was the largest source of canned food in Maine. The history also includes remarks about lobster. The crustaceans used to be quite large, and there were concerns about the supply lasting:

The packing lobsters has become so enormous that, with the present rate of canning, serious apprehensions are felt that the supply will not last many years longer. A few years ago it was not uncommon to catch lobsters weighing from ten to twenty pounds each; now the average weight is from three to six pounds, and growing less, thousands of which are caught weighing but little rising a pound each.

Between the late 1800s and early 1900s, some industries died out, and tourism began to take hold. Large hotels were constructed on Main Street and other areas of Bar Harbor. West Street in Bar Harbor saw construction of hotels, and in the early 1860s, there was an Indian encampment that offered tourists baskets and tours by canoe. Fish markets sprang up from the Bar Harbor Town Pier offering fresh fish and lobster straight from the boats.

Pollack in Eastport, Maine. *Courtesy of the Penobscot Marine Museum.*

Things were happening that poised Maine to be the top manufacturing area in the country. Water not only provided power but also produced ice. There was no electricity, so all refrigeration or freezers needed blocks of ice. Maine had cold water and ice, which was harvested and shipped all over the states and even to the Caribbean. According to the Maine Granite Museum, ice and granite were sometimes shipped together.

In 1874, 300,000 tons of ice were shipped from Maine, and the *History of Maine* asserts that ice promised "to be a fruitful source of income."

Manufacturing, commercial, mechanical and mining enterprises were rapidly being developed.

1873 Incomes for the State

Cotton manufactures	12½ million
Wool manufactures	7 million
Boots and shoes manufactures	9 million
Leather manufactures	4 million
Paper manufactures	3 million
Flour and grist mill products	2¼ million
Iron cast and forged	2 million
Machinery	2½ million
Edged tools	¾ million
Oil cloths	1½ million

Bricks	*½ million*
Fertilizers	*1 million*
Fisheries	*¾ million*
Lime	*2 million*
Forestry industry	*10 million*

In 1873, shipbuilding was one of the most important industries and would continue to be so.

Slate was shipped by the Maine Central Railroad.

These indicators show that Maine was growing, and the revenue from the fishing industry was not yet fully appreciated.

In 1860s, a large number of French Canadians came to the area for industry. Foods like poutine and ploys came too. Hoe cakes used only hot water, but as cows were imported you see butter or milk added to recipes because they were available.

Tourists are coming, the tourists are coming. Bar Harbor was becoming *the place* to visit, and tourists loved it. Well, except for possibly those smelly fish-packing facilities near where they stayed or where they were building their elaborate homes.

———◆———

RECIPES
Ploys

A French-Canadian pancake/crêpe/bread that uses only a few ingredients and can be used for breakfast with butter and molasses, at lunch as a wrap or with dinner as a flat bread

1 cup organic flour
2 cups organic buckwheat flour
2 teaspoons baking powder
Boiling water
Sunflower oil

Mix dry ingredients and add 2 cups boiling water. Use sunflower oil to grease the pan, and pour batter into the hot pan. Ploys were cooked on only one side, but I have often turned it over for more cooking. You can adjust the amount of boiling water for desired thickness.

• • •

Comforting Bread Pudding

1 loaf stale bread
1 quart milk
1–2 tablespoons butter, for greasing
4 eggs
1 ½ cups granulated sugar
2 tablespoons vanilla extract
1 cup raisins

Sauce
(Optional)

1 stick butter
1 cup confectionery sugar
4 tablespoons flavoring, like brandy

Crumble bread into a bowl and pour milk over it. Let it stand an hour. Preheat oven to 325 degrees. Grease a 9x15 pan with butter.

In a separate bowl, beat 3 eggs, sugar and vanilla. Stir into bread mixture and then stir in raisins. Pour into pan and bake until brown and set, about 1 hour and 10 minutes. Cool to room temperature. For the sauce, stir butter and confectionery sugar over double boiler. Beat remaining egg and whisk into sugar mixture. Keep whisking until cool and add flavoring.

• • •

Chicken Fricot, or Acadian Chicken and Dumplings

1 tablespoon organic olive oil
2 pounds boneless chicken thighs, skinned
1 medium carrot, chopped in ½-inch pieces
1 stalk celery, chopped in ½-inch pieces

1 medium onion, finely chopped
1 large potato, cut in 1-inch pieces
6 cups organic chicken stock
3 cloves garlic, chopped
3 sprigs of thyme
Salt and pepper

Dumplings
1 cup organic flour
1 teaspoon chopped thyme
2 teaspoons baking powder
½ teaspoon sea salt
½ cup milk

To make dumplings, mix dry ingredients and slowly add milk.

In oil, brown chicken on all sides and then remove thighs from pan. Cook carrot, celery and onion until tender and add potato. Shred chicken and add along with stock, garlic and thyme. Simmer, season to taste with salt and pepper and drop in dumplings, cooking until fluffy and tender.

• • •

Poutine
Poutine is a French-Canadian dish simply composed of french fries and white cheddar cheese curds with gravy poured over the top. It can be chicken gravy, beef or a mix of the two.

• • •

Blueberry Cobbler

1 ½ tablespoons cornstarch
¼ cup sugar
½ cup water

4 cups wild Maine blueberries
1 tablespoon butter
1 tablespoon lemon juice

Batter
½ cup flour
½ cup sugar
½ teaspoon baking powder
¼ teaspoon salt
2 tablespoons butter
1 egg, slightly beaten

Put the first four ingredients in a saucepan and cook until thickened (15 minutes). Then add butter and lemon juice. Pour into an 8-inch baking dish. Combine batter ingredients and drop spoonfuls on top of fruit. Bake at 400 degrees for 40 minutes.

• • •

Blueberry Grunt

1 quart blueberries
½ cup sugar
Zest of one lemon
1 tablespoon lemon juice
¼ cup water

Dumpling
1 ½ cups flour
2 teaspoons baking powder
1 ½ tablespoons sugar
1 tablespoon butter
⅔ cup milk

Heat first ingredients to boiling and simmer for five minutes while making the dumplings. For dumplings, mix dry ingredients and cut in butter. Add milk to make a soft dough. Drop by tablespoon into hot mixture and cover; cook for fifteen minutes and serve hot with optional ice cream or whipped cream.

• • •

Apple Oatmeal Crumble

4 organic Granny Smith apples, sliced
1 teaspoon tapioca flour or cornstarch
¼ cup sugar
½ teaspoon cinnamon

Topping
3 tablespoons unsalted butter
⅓ cup flour
⅓ cup brown sugar
⅛ teaspoon salt
⅓ cup oatmeal
½ cup finely chopped walnuts

Toss the first four ingredients together. For the topping, cut butter into flour, sugar and salt; then, add oatmeal and nuts. Cover apple mixture with topping and bake at 375 degrees for 35 minutes.

• • •

Date Pudding

8 tablespoons butter
1 ¼ cups sugar
2 eggs, beaten
1 cup milk
1 ½ tablespoons flour
1 ½ teaspoons baking powder
1 cup chopped walnuts

1 cup chopped dates
Whipped cream (optional)

Preheat the oven to 325 degrees. Cream butter and sugar; add eggs, milk, flour and baking powder and stir in walnuts and dates. Bake for 50 minutes. Makes 8 portions.

• • •

Colonial Flat Bread

With the popularity of a recipe and new ingredients, many adaptations appeared, such as using mashed sweet potatoes instead of cornmeal to make a different bread flavor.

1 cup mashed sweet potato
1 cup flour
Salt, to taste

Combine and flatten to cook on hot rocks in a fire.

• • •

Succotash

Succotash was often served with sliced tomatoes, biscuits and baked apples sweetened with maple syrup. The Scottish and Irish were some of the first to move into Downeast area.

2 cups lima beans
2¾ cups corn kernels
4 tablespoons butter
1 teaspoon organic sugar
½ teaspoon salt, some pepper to your taste
¾ cup heavy cream

Cook beans in boiling water about six minutes or put in microwave with a small amount of water for two minutes. Drain.

Place all ingredients into pot and cook on medium heat for five minutes.

• • •

Ambrosia Apple Pie

6 tart apples
Pastry for two-crust pie
2 tablespoons flour
½ cup sugar
½ cup brown sugar
1 teaspoon cinnamon
¼ teaspoon nutmeg
⅛ teaspoon salt
1 tablespoon lemon juice
3 tablespoons butter

Slice apples. Add water and simmer until tender. Cool. Put apples in pie shell. Combine remaining ingredients (except butter) and sprinkle over apples. Dot with butter. Moisten edges and put on top crust. Cut a few spots with knife to allow steam to rise. Bake at 450 for 10 minutes, then reduce oven temperature to 350 for 40 minutes or until crust is golden brown.

4

EARLY TOURISM AND GROWTH EXPANSION OF NEW FOODS AND INGREDIENTS

*New Industry Created Advances in Food Production,
Transportation and Preserving/Canning*

In the late 1800s, after the Civil War was over, transportation of food and people became easier and safer. Water power was an important method of transportation, just as frozen ice from winter rivers in Maine was cut and sold as an important industry. Homes, hotels and restaurants needed this ice for food preservation and making foods and drinks. Homes with iceboxes required a block of ice to keep foods safe. It was essential for homes to buy ice. Ice was also shipped to other areas of the country and even to the Caribbean. How did they do that? It is my understanding that the ice was shipped in sawdust. In the late nineteenth century, Downeast Maine began to see changes in transportation and recreation and food preservation.

Maine was poised to be the leading industrial state in the country, and that attracted many settlers. Things were happening. Roads were being built. Steam ships and railroads were built for more efficient transportation of manufactured goods. The nation took notice of opportunities in the manufacturing of textiles, and textiles became an important source of work for many Mainers. With the power from our many water sources, we were a major cotton manufacturer. Most of this industry was farther inland, but that industry had an effect on the foods in Downeast because of the new immigrants and the foods they brought. Downeast was building boats, harvesting seafood, establishing quarries and maintaining self-sufficient farms.

The lumber industry continued to expand, as wood was harvested near the coast but it was also available farther inland. Lumber proved to be

Tourists at a 1926 lobster boil in Hancock, Maine. *Courtesy of the Penobscot Marine Museum.*

profitable, and it was easy to find streams and rivers to move the logs. Ellsworth, Maine, became a thriving lumber town, as did other towns along the rivers. People in other towns like Stonington on the coast were living a simple seaside life and working in the fishing industry or in quarries.

In 1870, the only means of reaching Mount Desert Island was by steamship. The island was not connected to the mainland. You could take a steamship up the coast from Portland or Boston or you could take a steamship from Bangor down the Penobscot. Your other choice would be by stagecoach from a train in Bangor to Hancock Point and then by steamship to the island. Travel by steamship from Portland, Maine, increased to twice a week. Actually, the first steamships came from the southern New England coast to Bernard, a village in Tremont, on Mount Desert Island, and not Bar Harbor, according to Muriel Davisson of the Tremont Historical Society. Bernard had a steamboat landing and was a regular stop for a short period of time for tourists coming up the coast. The Tremont House in Bernard and the Mariner were hotels in the area

Lobstermen at Stonington, Maine. *Courtesy of the Penobscot Marine Museum.*

of Tremont. Stores like the Richardson store in Bass Harbor, places to eat were built and a movie theater was later established upstairs in the Reed Store. A major sardine cannery, the Underwood factory, brought workers to the area. It thrived for a while.

The demand for tourist transportation expanded the steamship routes to focus on Southwest Harbor and particularly on Bar Harbor. In 1884, it became possible to get closer to Mount Desert Island at Hancock Point by train and then connect to a steamship ferry. The "rusticators" came by the Maine Central Railroad and then arrived in Bar Harbor by steamship from the mainline. This made availability of the trains along the coast to Bar Harbor the easiest access for tourists from New York, Philadelphia and

Boston. It wasn't long before some of the wealthy brought their own train cars and servants.

They built their own magnificent twenty- and forty-room "cottages" with the amenities and servants they were used to having at home. Tourism was flourishing. Mostly local foods were served, such as seafood, as were typical foods like chicken. Sauces became the thing that would distinguish one hotel or restaurant's popularity over another. Private chefs of the wealthy cooked the foods of Philadelphia and New York and used local products. The Wabanaki set up stands along West Street to sell baskets and souvenirs to tourists. They took tourists on birchbark canoe rides. Fishermen sold freshly caught fish right from the pier, and there were fish markets that provided fresh fish to homes, hotels and tourists.

A major emphasis for people to come to visit Mount Desert Island in the late 1800s were paintings exhibited by Hudson River School artists like Frederic Church and Thomas Cole, who visited Mount Desert Island in the 1840s. The artists stayed at the Somes House in Somesville on Mount Desert Island.

Somes House was a first place for artists and travelers to stay in Somesville, Maine. *Courtesy of the Mount Desert Historical Society.*

Somes family at a picnic on the rocks. *Courtesy of the Mount Desert Historical Society.*

Seeing the natural beauty of Maine inspired rusticators, as they called themselves, to spend time in this beautiful area painted by the notable artists of the time.

The Seaside Inn was located in Seal Harbor on Mount Desert Island. It was built as a summer hotel, and it offered a varied menu. A rather formal menu from July 1904 offers salmon, which was in season, as well as native chicken and lamb. Lobster or fish were on every early menu alongside chicken and later steak.

The Seaside was torn down in 1964. Mount Desert Island became the place for the rich to go, and it rivaled the popular Newport resort area. It was *the* new place to visit. The Rodick House in Bar Harbor was built in 1866 with final expansion in 1881–82.

Hotels erected during that time were large, and the Rodick House hotel could hold six hundred guests. It was advertised as the largest hotel in Maine and was a social place for people to meet and mingle.

The hotel was torn down in 1906. A 1932 newspaper article in the *Bar Harbor Times* reflected on the past history of the hotel, which was torn down after a fairly short period of time. The Rodick House was advertised as having a ballroom that would hold 1,500 dancers; the 400 rooms would accommodate 500 to 600 guests; and a dining room could seat 700.

Expansion of hotels brought more people to the island and so did the Trenton Bridge, which was dedicated in 1920 and allowed the automobile,

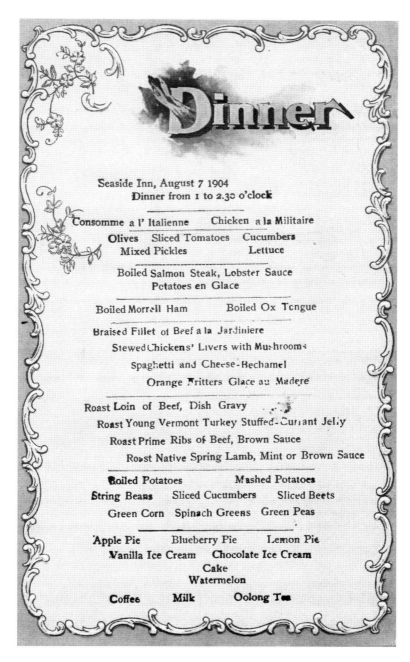

Dinner

Seaside Inn, August 7 1904
Dinner from 1 to 2.30 o'clock

Consomme a l' Italienne   Chicken a la Militaire
Olives   Sliced Tomatoes   Cucumbers
Mixed Pickles   Lettuce

Boiled Salmon Steak, Lobster Sauce
Potatoes en Glace

Boiled Morrell Ham   Boiled Ox Tongue

Braised Fillet of Beef a la Jardiniere
Stewed Chickens' Livers with Mushrooms
Spaghetti and Cheese-Bechamel
Orange Fritters Glace au Madere

Roast Loin of Beef, Dish Gravy
Roast Young Vermont Turkey Stuffed-Currant Jelly
Roast Prime Ribs of Beef, Brown Sauce
Roast Native Spring Lamb, Mint or Brown Sauce

Boiled Potatoes   Mashed Potatoes
String Beans   Sliced Cucumbers   Sliced Beets
Green Corn   Spinach Greens   Green Peas

Apple Pie   Blueberry Pie   Lemon Pie
Vanilla Ice Cream   Chocolate Ice Cream
Cake
Watermelon

Coffee   Milk   Oolong Tea

A 1904 menu from Seaside Inn shows what visitors were eating at that time. *Courtesy of the Mount Desert Historical Society.*

55

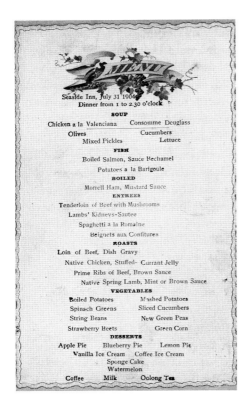

Left: Seaside Inn menu, 1904. A different day a different menu. *Courtesy of the Mount Desert Historical Society.*

Below: Rodick House advertised as the largest hotel in Maine. *Courtesy of the Mount Desert Historical Society.*

trucks and buses to reach Mount Desert Island. This meant that bringing the materials for building, supplies and foods was not dependent on the steamship.

The Kebo golf club in Bar Harbor was created in 1888. Kebo is the eighth-oldest club in the country and was the scene of many social events and even horse shows. President Taft played golf there, and it was a spot for society to mingle. There was a land boom in the 1880s, and magnificent homes were being built and gardens designed. Families like the Vanderbilts, Pulitzers and Rockefellers were some of the prominent visitors and residents here. Outings such as social picnics were recreational pastimes.

George Dorr, Charles Eliot and John D. Rockefeller had a vision to preserve land as a national park on Mount Desert Island. Acadia National Park had its beginning with lands donated by the Rockefellers, and the Rockefellers built unique individual stone bridges to create carriage roads. The bridges were created to get away from those new methods of transportation called "automobiles." All the bridges were different and made the carriage roads a place to take out your carriage and never see a car. Acadia National Park

Three women on a picnic. *Courtesy of the Mount Desert Historical Society.*

Views of Acadia National Park. *Author's collection.*

officially started in 1916, which also was the year that Rockefeller was declared the first billionaire and Kraft got a patent for processed cheese. There were no cars allowed on the carriage roads then, and today, no motored vehicles allowed on the carriage roads of Acadia National Park. Acadia National Park is considered one of the most beautiful parks in the world, and because it is a small national park, it has easy access to visit different parts of it. There are little parts of the park tucked away on various areas of the island. Acadia is a wonderful place; one can restore serenity, walk or hike and see beautiful vistas with little or no effort.

There is only one restaurant in the Acadia National Park, and it was grandfathered in. Jordan Pond House has an interesting food legacy. In the early days, the land was a lumbering area, and after a few owners, Jordan Pond House became a place where hikers would come in the afternoon for tea and popovers. It became a popular place to eat. In 1899, T.A. McIntire bought Jordan Pond House, and in 1915, he wrote a pamphlet about the land and restaurant:

> *In 1836 the first road was opened to Jordan Pond by William Bennett, who built a house and two mills. Three years later the Jordan brothers bought the property and operated the mills for many years, cutting and sawing the heavy growth of timber which covered the valleys and sides of the mountains—and the pond got its name. In 1847 they built the house*

which forms a part of the present Jordan Pond House. In 1852 a fire swept over the island leaving everything a blackened waste which was soon covered by the beginning of the present beautiful woods. In 1883, Mr. Charles T. Howell of Boston, one of the first to develop real estate in Bar Harbor, seeing the beauty of Jordan Pond and the surrounding country, bought the property just to have a place to which to drive with his friends for picnics. Delightful country pleasures, driving, walking, mountain climbing, boating and bathing.

He went on to describe the Jordan Pond House at the present day in 1915:

Crackling fire in the fireplace, it is an ideal place for lounging, music or playing games. Beside the music room there are private dining rooms each with a fireplace. Another attractive feature is dining on the porch. On pleasant days the broad verandas are arranged with tables at which all can sit and have the pleasure of eating out of doors, and on stormy days they afford a protected strolling place. Broiled live lobsters, broiled chicken and pop-popovers are Jordan Pond House specialties, and are served to perfection. The vegetables are delicious, brought in from the garden every day.

In 1931, Jordan Pond House advertised dinners, lunches and teas. The ads also said there were art goods and novelties. The food advertised was "Broiled Lobster and Chicken. Our famous Popovers and Home Grown Vegetables, Pure Fruit Home Made Ice Cream." T.A. McIntire lived from 1869 to 1954. He and his wife ran the Jordan Pond House from 1895 for fifty years. In 1950, Acadia Corporation received the permission to run the Jordan Pond House after the McIntires to benefit the Acadia National Park. The 1950 menu offers sirloin steak for $4.75, and lobster salad at $2.75 and Lobster Newburg for $4.50 were added to the menu. Popovers became a part of the island's history. Mrs. Nellie McIntire's handwritten recipe for popovers may be seen at the Bar Harbor Historical Society. Her recipe for twelve popovers is as follows and was the basis for their restaurant.

12 Popovers
Beat 4 eggs into bowl. Best dry—impossible to beat too much. High ¾ cup whole milk poured into eggs along with 2 cups sifted flour with pinch of salt. Beat to smooth batter with mixing spoon.
    Add 1¼ cups milk mech 2 min gradually. When batter is thin enough use Rotary Beater. Beat until Bubbly. Use Pillsbury' Best Bake at 425

Jordan Pond House.
*Courtesy of the Acadia
Corporation.*

*Tilt in Tin, to dry 40 min
Grease + flour tins + have cold
Put knife blade in door to hold door open a tiny bit*

The Jordan Pond House burned down once, but it was rebuilt in 1979 and still serves popovers and tea as well as ice cream and a full menu.

The Acadia Corporation ran the Jordan Pond House for years, and it now makes the McIntires' famous popovers at the historic Asticou Inn in Northeast Harbor on Somes Sound.

Other things were happening in other parts of the country that would have a profound effect on industry and food in Maine. Around this time, the first electric refrigerator was introduced; it would eventually lead to the end of the ice industry.

While the early tourists stayed in private homes at first, hotels soon followed. They were large and attracted more people. The hotels set the social scene, and it attracted even more tourists.

Asticou Inn. *Author's collection*.

View from Asticou Inn porch looking toward Northeast Harbor. *Author's collection*.

Now that train travel opened up to the coast, it made travel to Bar Harbor easy. The tourist population soared. Bar Harbor became the shortest and easiest destination on the island. The Bar Harbor Pier welcomed visitors, with only a short distance to their hotels.

Expansion of hotels brought more people to the island, and the tourist population wanted to be in Bar Harbor, as it was near the social scene and the main portions of Acadia National Park and close to the transportation from the Bar Harbor Pier. Hotels came and went; restaurants came and went.

When the railroads first started coming up the coast, they were mostly concerned with shipment of goods, so passengers would have whatever food they had prepared in their lunch baskets or what was picked up at brief station stops. Sometimes, the trains would have a twenty-to-twenty-five-minute dining stop where a restaurant would have everything ready to quickly serve a train full of people.

In 1887, a new railway composed of parlor and dining cars could connect Boston to Bar Harbor steamship ferries with no change of trains. It was a fashionable way to travel and advertised to arrive in nine hours. In 1888, the Mount Desert Limited was advertised as the fastest train in New England. It would travel from the Hancock Point ferry to Boston in seven hours and forty-five minutes. Long-distance train travel became elegant, and in the early 1900s, the train might serve consommé, salmon with hollandaise or soufflés. Of course, fine wines or champagne would accompany the meals. Trains became the premier way to travel. The food was prepared by chefs on the train. Things changed with the introduction of the car, namely, an easier way to reach Mount Desert Island. During the early 1920s, there was train service from Washington, Philadelphia and New York. The glamour of trains continued during the summer tourist seasons, with the wealthy and well known traveling by train and some having their own personal train car. As Arthur Dubin reported in his book *Some Classic Trains*, "Complete tea service was available from buffet for patrons of chairs with fringed seat cushions in this gorgeous parlor car." Slowly, things changed when a causeway was built to connect the island to the mainland. The development caused a decrease in passengers wanting to use the ferries, and a bus took passengers from the train in Ellsworth to Bar Harbor. Roads were built as the automobile made travel easier with the connection by road to Mount Desert Island. Steamship service diminished and ceased operations in 1931.

Later, after World War II, the trains were looking toward economy, not elegance. The onboard staff would prepare canned or frozen foods. Quick meals and snacks became the norm. Train companies were looking at the bottom line because of fewer riders, and the transport of goods was down due to transportation by trucks.

The Tremont Historical Society and Museum is now located in the former Richardson store. Located in Bass Harbor, the society has information about this important fishing area and a major sardine cannery. The Underwood sardine factory was a thriving business in the early to mid-1900s. It closed, but the building still stands and was redeveloped as luxury condominiums.

Muriel Davisson of the Tremont Historical Society gave me several handwritten recipes from the late 1800s and early 1900s. These are her grandmother Lovina Ethel Joyce Moore's recipes. Lovina was born in 1878 and married about 1897. She and her husband lived on Gott's Island and ran the general store and post office on the island. Gott's Island is one of many small islands off Mount Desert Island in Downeast Maine. Lovina used ledger books to make a cookbook and wrote her recipes in addition to pasting in copies of newspaper articles that had interesting cooking ideas.

Muriel remembers her grandmother's cooking well; Lovina used some recipes so often she didn't write them down. Lovina's recipe for corned hake was an old favorite. It is an easy and different meal that was very popular at that time.

Corned hake is a simple recipe for salted hake, which is a type of cod, and potatoes with salt pork. A more modern version is at the end of the chapter. The idea is that someone would boil potatoes, and when they were just tender, you would add half as much hake to the boiling water. Drain, maybe add a little pepper and put on dinner plates, then mash fish and potato together on the plate. The crispy pork scraps from frying the salt pork would be poured over the top. Salted hake would be soaked in water overnight. If the fish was still too salty, the water would be drained and replaced with fresh water for a longer soaking.

Lovina Ethel Joyce Moore recipe book. Lovina was born in 1878 and lived on Gott's Island. *Courtesy of granddaughter Muriel Davisson, Tremont.*

A similar recipe shows up in an old Nova Scotia recipe book using salted cod. Lovina's family was from Nova Scotia, so there may or may not be a connection. It was a popular dish. The Nova Scotia recipe called for cod, salt pork and onions poured over the salt cod and potatoes.

Another memory from Muriel Davisson was when her grandmother would make yeast bread. She would tear off a few chunks and fry them, probably in lard. The preparation was similar to the cooking of Indian fry bread, but she made up her own name for them and called them "Huff Chuffs."

Here are excerpts from that ledger book. Lovina had with a note that the cake was good next to the recipe

Blueberry Cake

1 teaspoon baking powder or 2 teaspoons cream of tartar and 1 of soda
Rub together ¼ cup of butter and 1 cup sugar
1 beaten egg
1 cup milk
Add the flour and 2 cups of berries well flavored.

This recipe does show the change from cream of tartar and baking soda to an easier form called baking powder. Baking powder was developed in the mid-1800s. The recipe probably called for two teaspoons of cream of tartar and one teaspoon baking soda mixed together, and then one teaspoon for the recipe was taken out, as that would be the equivalent of one teaspoon baking powder. Baking powder was invented as an easier way for homemakers to measure. The cream of tartar and baking soda were already combined. Cream of tartar is the remnants of wine in a cask and has been used for thousands of years to leaven breads. If you read the labels of baking powder today, you will see manufacturers are using cornstarch instead of cream of tartar. Cream of tartar is still sold today, so you can make your own with a ratio of two cream of tartar to one baking soda.

What were the popular styles of cooking at the time? Lovina had an excerpt from the Department of Commerce Bureau of Fisheries Economic Circular no. 12, issued March 24, 1914, *Sea Mussel: What They Are and How to Cook Them*. The circular cost five cents and offered eighteen different recipes.

It suggested ways of cooking that were particularly popular. If you could make the following sauces, you could use them not only for mussels but also for fish and other shellfish. Sauces could be used to fit a number of fish and seafood preparations and would complement techniques like steaming, roasting and frying. Different preparations include mussels cooked in a broth, placed in a chowder, croquettes, fritters, creamed or with sauces such as Provençal, bourguignonne, Newburg, marinara and mornay. These were the sauces that were being prepared in great restaurants and were suggested to be possible for the aspiring cook.

STEAM-POWERED SHIPS REPLACED SAILING ships for passengers as well as for fishermen. Catching fish was easier with steam power and even easier and more profitable with diesel power.

There were mixed feelings about the introduction of the car on the island. Cars were not allowed on the carriage roads and still aren't, but they did make the island more accessible.

The train flourished for a number of years, but the number of passengers was slowly decreasing. More tourists were arriving in their own cars.

Henry Ford was one of the early rusticators who came to Mount Desert Island, and his son, Edsel, had a home in Seal Harbor Maine called Skylands. It is now owned by Martha Stewart.

Most people associate Henry Ford with invention of the automobile assembly line, but Ford was an early pioneer in the area of soy production. He felt that the soybean was the possible answer to many problems in the world, and promoted its use in cooking, healthcare and car parts. He thought that the cow was a poor choice to get milk. He asked, "Why feed cows and then have to milk them when you could just have soy milk?" He had an experimental station in Dearborn, Michigan, where he studied soy food properties and introduced an all-soy menu at the 1934 Exposition in Chicago. He also felt that the automobile industry could benefit from the soybean to make car parts and shellac. The 1908 Model T Ford was the first automobile to have parts that were grown from soy plants and made from ground soy. Ford had worked for Thomas Edison, and they became lasting friends when he left to start his own company. They both wintered in Fort Meyers, Florida, in homes next to each other. He felt that "one should go to the earth for solutions."

MENU of Dinner Served at Ford Exhibit
Century of Progress
August 17, 1934

TOMATO JUICE SEASONED WITH SOY BEAN SAUCE
SALTED SOY BEANS
CELERY STUFFED WITH SOY BEAN CHEESE
PUREE OF SOY BEAN

SOY BEAN CRACKER
SOY BEAN CROQUETTES WITH TOMATO SAUCE
BUTTERED GREEN SOY BEANS
PINEAPPLE RING WITH SOY BEAN CHEESE AND SOY BEAN DRESSING
SOY BEANS BREAD WITH SOY BEAN RELISH
SOY BEAN MACAROONS
APPLE PIE (SOY BEAN CRUST)
COCOA WITH SOY BEAN MILK
SOY BEAN COFFEE
ASSORTED SOY BEAN COOKIES
SOY BEAN CAKES
ASSORTED SOY BEAN CANDY

———•———

RECIPES

Modern Version of Lovina's Corned Hake for Those without Salt Pork

Cod with Potatoes and Bacon

Maine white potatoes
1 pound cod
Bacon, fried crispy

Peel and cut up potatoes to have the amount twice as much as the fish. Boil potatoes until just tender, add cod and continue boiling until fish is white in color. Drain and place on individual plate. Mash fish and potatoes together, drizzle a little hot bacon fat over the plate and sprinkle with bacon pieces. Pepper added to individual taste at table.

• • •

Another Recipe from Lovina's Ledger

Vanilla Ice Cream

1 quart milk
½ cup flour
1 cup sugar
2 eggs

Let the milk come to a boil. Beat together the flour, sugar and eggs. Add to hot milk and cook 20 minutes, stirring often. Set aside to cool. When cool, add 1 quart cream, 1 cup sugar and vanilla to flavor.

• • •

Caramel Ice Cream

Same as vanilla preparation but cook small cup of sugar on stove until brown and add to boiling mixture. Then add the 1 quart cream.

Makes about 3 quarts

• • •

Model T Crackers by Ford's Personal Chef Jan Willemse in Book *Cooking for Henry*
(*Mr. Ford's Favorite*)

Ford's chef Jan Willemse wrote a soy cookbook called Cooking for Henry *and gave this recipe as Ford's favorite cracker, using a Model T Ford hubcap as a cookie cutter.*

Model T Crackers

1 cup pastry flour
1 cup soybean flour
1 cup whole wheat flour

2 tablespoons baking powder
1 tablespoons salt
2 cups sugar
1 cup soft soybean margarine
1 cup soy milk (or regular milk)
1 tablespoon wheat germ

Preheat oven to 350 degrees. Mix all flours, baking powder, salt, sugar and margarine together, rubbing it between your hands as you would for piecrust. Add all the milk and mix a little. Place dough on work table; roll it out ¹/8-inch thick. Sprinkle with some wheat germ. Cut with clean Model T hubcap (or 2- or 3-inch cookie cutter). Place on baking sheet; prick with fork 3 or 4 times. Bake for about 10–12 minutes. Serve with soup salad or cheese. Yields about 4 dozen crackers.

• • •

Popover Recipe

There are many recipes for popovers, but I have included the one I use in my classes. It is simple, and it works. There are a few basis steps to remember. Use a good nonstick pan, have all ingredients at room temperature and preheat the oven.

Popovers. *Author's collection.*

• • •

Ambrosia's Popovers

3 organic eggs
1 ½ cups whole milk
1 ½ cups of organic flour

Mix ingredients and fill each cup ½ to ⅔ full of an ungreased nonstick popover pan. Place in the middle of the oven and cook for around 25 minutes. The popovers should be puffed up and golden brown. Don't open the oven a lot, as the popover rises because of the steam from the mixture and, like a soufflé, won't be successful if you open the oven too much or if you do not serve right away. Note: I use all organic ingredients when possible.

Variations of flavor could be made to the recipe for different meals. You could add dill to the batter for a wonderful touch or any light herb that fits with your menu. You don't want to add anything heavy, as that will hold the batter down and it won't rise well. Popovers are good for breakfast, lunch and dinner. Different butters and preserves make it a bread that is as easy as going to the store and more versatile. Butter with a hint of molasses, mashed blueberries or maple syrup added are great ways to accompany popovers and to make breakfast special.

• • •

Watercress Salad

Watercress
Tomato
Cucumber
Onion
Olive oil
Vinegar

Chop all the vegetables small and add olive oil and vinegar.

• • •

Brandy Snaps

1 stick unsalted butter, softened
¼ cup organic confectioner's sugar
5 teaspoons maple syrup
1 teaspoon molasses
½ cup flour
½ teaspoon ginger
⅛ teaspoon nutmeg
¼ cup brandy
2 teaspoons finely grated lemon peel

Mix first 4 ingredients and then the remainder. Bake at 350 on parchment 6–8 minutes.

• • •

Standing Rib Roast

Bake in oven at 500 for twenty minutes, then reduce to 350, using thermometer for preferred temperature: 130–140 rare, 150–160 medium, 160–170 well done. When oven is turned to 350 expect about 25 minutes per pound for medium, 30 minutes per pound for well done.

No basting needed or grate, as you place rib side down, creating a natural rack.

• • •

Yorkshire Pudding

½ cup beef drippings
2 eggs
1 cup milk
1 cup flour
¼ teaspoon salt

After beef is cooked, keep ½ cup of drippings and put them in a circular or square oven-proof pan. Beat eggs with milk and slowly add to flour/salt mixture to form a batter. Heat dripping until hot and then add the egg/flour/milk mixture. This is a relative of the popover and should be cooked at 375 for about 20 minutes.

• • •

Horseradish Sauce

¼ cup bottled horseradish, drained
1 tablespoon white wine vinegar
1 teaspoon sugar
¼ teaspoon dry mustard
½ cup heavy cream
Salt and pepper

Mix well.

• • •

Needhams

Needhams were invented in the late 1800s, and the chocolate-coated coconut candies were made with potatoes. They called for canning wax as an ingredient in the chocolate in early recipes. This is a more modern version.

¾ cup warm mashed potatoes
2 pounds of organic confectionery sugar or to taste
1 stick unsalted butter
14 ounces flaked organic coconut

Chocolate Coating

2 teaspoons vanilla
2 packages unsweetened chocolate
¼ cup sugar (optional)

Mix first four ingredients and form into small balls. For chocolate dipping, take unsweetened chocolate and add up to ¼ cup sugar if desired. Melt with vanilla in top of a double boiler. Dip balls in chocolate and place on parchment paper to cool.

• • •

Lobster Newburg

2 cups lobster
2 tablespoons butter
¼ teaspoon salt
1 dash cayenne
3 tablespoons sherry
3 egg yolks
1 cup light cream

Heat all ingredients but yolks and cream, then mix yolks with cream and add to lobster. Stir until thick. Serve on buttered toast.

5

THE ABUNDANCE OF LOCAL FOODS AND THE LURE OF A BEAUTIFUL PLACE LIKE ACADIA NATIONAL PARK CREATES A DIVERSE MENU FOR TOURISTS AND LOCALS

In the early 1900s, steamship passengers were declining. In 1925, cars were on Mount Desert Island, making it more accessible for more tourists. Also, passengers could disembark a train in Ellsworth and be transported by buses to Bar Harbor. The seclusion of this wealthy resort area was opening up to a wider audience. Roads, trains and travel put food in a new light. Acadia was now a national park. The Rockefellers had bridges designed to have carriage roads built so people didn't have to be around those new-fangled automobiles, but they were becoming the new way of life. The famous and wealthy built homes here. Presidents and well-known visitors came. It was the place to be. Cars made it affordable for the average American to come to Downeast Maine. Catering to the wealthy brought jobs to the area. The rusticators came to the area to experience living a simple life but then wanted the luxuries they were used to and that they could afford.

As large estates were built, the owners needed caretakers and staff to manage the homes. The Pulitzers were early rusticators in Downeast Maine. They hired Katherine Richards and her husband. Kay was born in Machiasport in 1914 and had four sisters. Kay was the head housekeeper for the Pulitzer family for thirty-two years. Her husband was caretaker. She gave me the recipe that she used to make chowder for the Pulitzer family when they arrived in Bar Harbor. She would tell me stories of Joseph Pulitzer calling to tell Kay that the family was coming up to Maine and asking if she could have chowder ready. Her recipe shows a small change from the usual old Downeast traditional recipe, which would have called for salt pork instead of the butter used in

Thunderhole in Acadia National Park. *Author's collection.*

Kay's version. It is a great recipe that is simple, easy to have the ingredients on hand and freezes well. It is at the end of this chapter.

Food shipments continued to get easier. Homeowners could keep food fresh with new electric refrigerators. Refrigerators replaced the icebox, which used blocks of ice for keeping food cold.

The tourism-based expansion brought many jobs and small businesses. The School Street Market started in 1936 and was one of many small markets and small dairies on Mount Desert Island.

Vern McFarland owned the School Street Market on School Street in Bar Harbor; it was financed by his father, Sanford. Sanford had owned a small dairy farm in Salisbury Cove in Bar Harbor. Sanford McFarland sold the dairy farm after World War II, and he worked with his son in the market. It was all about personalized service and high-quality foods. Markets such as Vern's store had loyal customers. Soft drink companies like Coke and Pepsi would send promotional items from TV programs like *Kit Carson*, a popular cowboy show, to the stores to encourage people to buy their products.

Small markets began to decline because of self-service stores. In an April 26, 1962 article in the *Bar Harbor Times*, LaRue Spiker wrote about why Vern McFarland was still able to operate his market after twenty-six years even though the trend was going toward the supermarket and trading stamps:

> *About 60% of the market's business is done through the delivery service. The customer calls the market and tells them what she wants. The order is put together and then delivered to her home. If no one is there perishables such as ice cream are placed in the refrigerator.*
>
> *Some of the market's customers of 20 years' standing have never been inside the store, having always done all their buying over the phone. McFarland, by virtue of his long dealings with them, sometimes knows their needs better than they do themselves.*
>
> *The market is one of the few places where the customer can get meat cut to order rather than the pre-cut and packaged.*
>
> *The business has also been maintained by extending a friendly helping hand to its customers—a service seldom found in in business relationships today. Not infrequently the delivery man stops to help a woman put up a storm door, do an errand for her, or take her to the hospital. To younger people who have grown up in a strictly commercial age, this may sound a little silly. But it is something over and beyond good business practice. It is a kind of friendliness that America is losing and will be much the poorer for when it is completely driven out by commercialized hurly-burly.*

Vern McFarland. Small markets and dairies flourished before the grocery store and supermarket came along. *Courtesy of the* Bar Harbor Times.

Refrigerators were common by the 1950s, and most people had one. This helped if you were stocking up on food at a new self-service grocery store. In 1916, Piggly Wiggly became the first self-service grocery store in the country. In Downeast, the A&P chain expanded into this area and took over the customers of many of the small markets.

A&P history shows that it started small. Gilman and Company sold their company to the founder of A&P, George Hartford, and the company started by selling only coffee and tea. The second step was bread, and then the focus expanded to have a full self-service store for shoppers. Feeling that it could reduce prices by buying direct, the company grew to be the largest grocery in the United States from 1915 to 1975. The Great Atlantic and Pacific Tea Company filed for bankruptcy in 2015 The A&P was succeeded by Don's Shop and Save, and the School Street Market closed. Vern McFarland joined Don's Shop and Save and was front-end manager until he retired. Vern would always ask friends and family if we needed any lobster or crab meat when he went to his favorite source for seafood on the quiet side of Mount Desert Island. He dipped the lobster in apple cider vinegar. He never ate butter with lobster and served it with a special presentation when he cooked it.

It was common for locals to make fun of the wealthy, but the islanders realized that the money brought into the area was how they made a living.

The locals saw the elaborate entertaining and fancy balls that the wealthy enjoyed and they were not invited to attend. They decided to start their own ball. As a spoof and way to unwind from the season of dealing with wealthy tourists, a group of locals created the 40 Hayseeders Ball. The 40 Hayseeders Ball started in the late 1800s, and each year's invitation offers a glimpse into the issues members experienced in the preceding year. Each year, an invitation would be sent out for this exclusive event with commentary about whatever had happened locally or in world events. It is an interesting look at how a small area looked at world events from a central and sometimes humorous view. No wealthy summer people or people from away were invited. The food served at this annual ball included dried fish, donuts and a sharp cheddar fondly called rat cheese. The 40 Hayseeders Ball continues today, and the menu is the same.

It wasn't just the rich and famous who came to live in this area of Maine. Downeast Maine attracted authors, artists and people who wanted to live the simple life. They felt that this area was what they were looking for to enjoy and appreciate life.

Scott and Helen Nearing were both raised in wealthy homes. She was raised vegetarian, and he adopted Helen's food tastes after he met her.

Presentation of lobster. *Author's collection.*

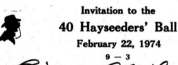

Invitation to the
40 Hayseeders' Ball
February 22, 1974

9 — 3

Now Gramp's been ailing some of late.
Grandma says it's "Watergate".
Then Spiro Agnew came on strong,
claims he ain't done nothin wrong.
Grampa said "Now that one's afixin
to move right in on Richard Nixon.

But when facts and figures hit the fan,
Spiro jumped the gun and ran.
Then one day in the County Seat
Gramp heard the Russians bought our wheat;
but when the Arabs stopped our oil,
that made Gramp's blood pressure boil.
He said "I'm keeping out of harm
and heading back out to the farm,
where I can live as people should,
where folks heat their homes and cook by wood".

The cellar's full and so's the shed;
but now he dast not go to bed,
for fear some chicken thievin nut

will try to heist the wood he's cut.
He's got the cook stove bolted down
in case some cockeyed guy from town
finds out what they're selling for
and tries to move her out the door.
"Old Betsey's" loaded with rocksalt
and if they don't stop when he says "halt"
they'll be standing up to eat
with a charge of rocksalt in their seat.

So let the Arabs keep their oil,
let's put the coffee on to boil
and set a spell and cogitate
on Nixon, Agnew, Watergate.
But thinking backward's not much fun
so when our cogitating's done,
let's look ahead and see what's due
to happen February 22.

It's the 80th Hayseed Ball by Gosh!

Notis

Bring this along and show it to the officer at the doer and its your pass out check to. The orchestree will play the first walse at nine o'clock and we'll hold the grand march at 9:30. Same rools will prevail as in the past. We hope this one will be a doozer. This will be the 80th. Gosh All Hemlock!

40 Hayseeders invitation, 1974. *Courtesy of the 40 Hayseeders.*

They came to Harborside, Maine, in 1952 and started living off the land. They planted crops seasonally and to carry them through the winter. The Nearings were an inspiration to many in living off the land. They wrote many books, including perhaps the best known, *Living the Good Life.* Their speaking engagements and books were their source of income. They didn't sell any of their food at local markets but used the crops to survive. I had an interview with Warren Berkowitz, who is still associated with the farm, and his wife was even more involved with both Scott and Helen while they were alive. Berkowitz said the Nearings never ate meat, fish or dairy. They built a stone house by hand. Their cooking was very simple, and Helen used vegetable oil for cooking. They mostly ate salad, soups and stews that tasted similar. They would eat bread if they were out to dinner, but they never bought or made bread at home. They did buy grains to add to soups and always bought peanut butter and popcorn. A salad might be carrot, radish, swiss chard, lettuce and anything else in season.

The soups/stews were all similar, vegetables with possible additions of beans and peas. They might have a potato baked in the oven, but Helen

Rainbow swiss chard. *Author's collection.*

Nearing mentioned once to a dinner host that mashed potatoes were too much work. Interestingly they had popcorn at every meal. Scott liked fruit such as apples and bananas for dessert, but Helen liked ice cream and would take the opportunity to take some for friends if she were invited to dinner at a friend's house. Some 80 percent of what they ate came from the garden, including tomatoes, corn, squash, turnips, parsnips and other vegetables that would keep through the winter. Helen and Scott both had interesting life stories, and Warren Berkowitz mentioned that their relationship was a romance. Their story lives on at the Good Life Center, and their work is well known in the United States and worldwide.

Scott Nearing was a mentor to Eliot and Barbara Coleman, who bought land from the Nearings and have an organic farm called 4 Seasons Farm. Daughter Ella now runs the farm and mentors others. 4 Seasons sells the excess of its crops year-round in farmer's markets. Ella said she remembered her mother making brown bread and beans and custard. She makes custards for her children. Her father always requests filet, peas, mashed potatoes and lemon meringue pie for his birthday.

Summer berries. *Author's collection.*

Ella said that her father suggested they get a cow, but the rest of the family voted him down. Barbara Coleman is a landscape architect from New England, and Eliot was from New Jersey. They have written a number of books. When I asked an intern from France why she had come to this farm to work for the summer, she said, referring to Eliot Coleman, "Because he's a rock star." They were harvesting charlotte potatoes.

Nature's Circle is another organic farm, near Houlton, Maine, and it grows and packs potatoes and other root vegetables. When I visited Nature's Circle farm, workers were harvesting potatoes and squash.

Restaurants were needed to feed many tourists and local patrons. Many restaurants, as well as hotels, have changed, been demolished, gone out of business or changed ownership. Tourist wanted local foods as well as the foods they liked at home. Restaurants and hotels usually have lobster and fish on their menus. They want to please everyone, so other alternatives like chicken or beef are common as well.

Fish markets made buying seafood right off the boat possible, but some felt it could be rather smelly. Controversy over locals needing income and the

Harvesting potatoes at Eliot Coleman's farm. *Author's collection.*

Maine potatoes. *Author's collection.*

Squash being harvested in the fall at an organic farm. *Author's collection.*

wealthy wanting waterfront homes away from seafood processing plants created long-term problems and would have a lasting effect on the fishing industry.

Around 1950, Gorton's fish stick went on the market. Fish was frozen in a block, sliced with a band saw and then cut into small sticks. What a boon to the family trying to get children to eat fish. They got a Good Housekeeping Institute approval. It was easy to just heat up the frozen breaded stick—no fish smell and easy, time-saving preparation. By 1970, the U.S. production of fish sticks had tripled.

Clarence Birdseye had studied how people in Greenland were able to eat vegetables all year round by freezing them. In 1925, he founded General Seafoods Company. He then turned to freezing fruits and vegetables. Freezing brought about factory ships where fishing, processing and freezing were all done onboard. Markets and grocery stores could keep foods longer but needed more space for frozen foods and, of course, canned goods.

The crab industry was doing well. Crabs in Downeast are cooked by steaming; then they are picked, and the meat is packaged for sale. The pieces are smaller than you might find in the center of the country along the coast. Chowders, bisques and crab rolls are popular foods, as are crab cakes.

Canned goods were making life easier. People could store food and use it at their leisure instead of having to shop often. Foods that were once only available fresh, dried or smoked were now easily available in cans and frozen. The modern methods flourished in Downeast as they did in the rest of the country. Canned goods were convenient, and they were handy to keep for preparation at a moment's notice. Soups were now available in cans and were the base of numerous dishes. It was easy cooking in a society that was beginning to see both parents working outside the home. Packaged cake mixes and Jell-O fit right in.

Aspics are composed with gelatin and usually have vegetables, fruit or seafood layered in the design. They were often used for more formal entertaining. These creative, artistic foods were created by a process of layering the food in a gelatin mold. With the invention of Jell-O, suddenly it was easier for the average family to make dessert that children liked, and they could be as artistic or creative as they saw fit. It was a perfect food to bring to a potluck dinner. Gelatin still has a place in cooking, and if you try

Crab pickers at Machiasport Canning Company on C.H. Rich's Wharf, McKinley, Maine, 1960. *Courtesy of the Southwest Harbor Library.*

this recipe, you can also use up your leftover coffee. Try it—the flavors of the coffee and cream with a touch of curry are surprising good.

———•———

Recipes

Dark Coffee Gelatin

2 cups of dark hot coffee, with ⅛ cup sugar dissolved in ¼ cup of water
1 ½ teaspoons unflavored gelatin
2 teaspoons vanilla

Combine hot coffee with other ingredients and chill for six hours or until firm.

Topping
Up to ¼ cup dark brown sugar
1 cup chilled heavy cream
¼ teaspoon curry

Whip the cream and sugar; add curry.

White Sauce
2 tablespoons flour
2 tablespoons butter
1 cup warm/hot milk
Salt and pepper to taste

Heat the flour and butter in a pan, making sure the mixture doesn't get brown. When the mixture has cooked, add cup of hot milk, more if needed. Let mixture continue to cook and thicken. Add salt and pepper to taste.

Cheese Sauce
Add ¼ cup of cheddar cheese at the end and let it melt into the mixture.

• • •

Kay's Chowder Recipe for the Pulitzer Family

Giving you exact measurements depends on the pan and the amount of chowder you want to make. It is really about proportions. Use the same amount of onion, potato and the fish or other flavor ingredient.

Butter enough that the onions are swimming in the butter
Onions, minced
White Maine potatoes, peeled and cut in small pieces about half the size of the top joint of your small finger
Water, enough to just cover potatoes
Haddock or cod fish, cut in a little larger than bite-size pieces, as they will shrink some while cooking.
(Flavor could be fish, corn, lobster, clams, scallops, shrimp, mussels, fiddleheads, etc.)
Whole milk to just cover fish
White pepper
Salt
Cream to drizzle over final chowder to make basically a thin sheet on top the chowder

The pot should be at medium low to low heat, and the temperature doesn't change during any of the cooking. Melt butter and add onions. Add more butter until the onions are just swimming in the butter. Cook until translucent.

Add potatoes to pan and just cover with water. No stirring should be done, just add as a layer and it needs to be white potatoes. Cook until just tender and then add the fish.

Cover fish with enough whole milk so that the fish will be covered but not so much liquid that it will make the chowder too thin. At this point add a few pats of butter and lightly add salt and white pepper. Cook until fish is white and then add a light topping of cream to the top layer. Enjoy right away, or set aside in refrigerator for up to a few days or freeze in small glass freezer bowls with lids.

*Sometimes, older recipe versions use salt pork instead of butter, but Kay's recipe did not, and it is a recipe with ingredients that may be found wherever you happen to be.

• • •

Asparagus Casserole

2 cups milk
2 eggs
Bread (about 2 slices), torn into small pieces
Asparagus
Grated cheddar (about 2 cups)

Beat milk and eggs until foamy. Layer bread, asparagus and cheese. Repeat and then pour milk mixture over it. Cook in 350 oven for 30 minutes and cheese is bubbly on top.

6

EFFECTS OF CHANGE LIKE PROHIBITION, WARS, FADS AND THE BOTTOM LINE

The New England Historical Society suggests that the reason the Pilgrims landed near Plymouth Rock was that they were running out of alcohol and were afraid of the backlash that it would cause with the passengers and crew. The colonists drank a lot of alcohol, and they knew how to make more. Alcohol can be made from a variety of bases. Corn, barley, apples, pumpkins, parsnips and very well-done baked cornbread were some of them. The Native Americans had made alcohol from corn and showed the new colonists their methods. The historical society explained how malt was made:

> *In the home breweries of the poorer people a "malt" made of Indian corn was used. The process of "malting" corn had been learned from the Indians, as the colonists had been unable to make a satisfactory malt from it. The natives sprouted the corn in the ground, drilling it thickly in rows. When the corn had been in the ground about fourteen days and had developed a sprout two or three inches long, it was dug up, root and all, washed clean and dried. Beer made from this was said to be "wholesome, pleasant."*

We were the first. Yes, Maine passed the first legislation to outlaw the sale of alcohol, with the exception for industrial and medical purposes. Maine's Governor Neal Dow was a Quaker. He disliked alcohol for reasons of the temperance movement and also felt slavery and rum were intertwined. He was founder of the Maine Temperance Society and instrumental in getting the Twenty-Eight Gallon Law passed in 1846. Basically, consumers had to buy twenty-eight gallons of alcohol at a time, which was good for the rich, but the average person couldn't afford that. Doctors were exempt. Places selling single drinks were shut down. Those selling single drinks were called "tippling shops." Evidently, Dow was purchasing alcohol and storing it in city hall to be distributed to doctors, but the population stormed city hall and felt Dow was breaking his own law.

In 1851, Maine was the first state to prohibit the manufacturing and sale of alcohol. Other areas were drinking with their meals, but Maine became a model for the Woman's Christian Temperance Union and others in their goal for national Prohibition. At that time, women were not allowed to drink or go to taverns, and men were working in mostly hard labor jobs. The law was repealed in 1858, and then it was made as permanent as Maine could make it in 1885 when it became part of the state constitution. After the biggest political opponent of alcohol died, the state worked to make a more livable solution. Several counties were given the ability to regulate their own liquor dealers, and areas could charge a nuisance fee so the county would get to make revenue. There was encouragement for drinking places to be low key and hidden away from the public as much as possible. The law was repealed in 1856, but new restrictions on alcohol were instituted. Maine's legislation became a basis for national Prohibition from 1920 to 1933.

In 1920, the Volstead Act became law and National Prohibition began.

Other areas of the country had until 1920 before Prohibition would be implemented. In 1921, President Harding signed the Willis Campbell Act, which prohibited doctors from prescribing beer or alcohol. Prohibition lasted until 1933. Governor Percival Baxter came into office and stressed that law enforcement would crack down on those who had been engaged in the alcohol trade and doing it very successfully.

It was difficult to regulate. Everyone grew apples and corn. If you were a cook who had a problem of overcooking cornbread, you could have become a successful producer of alcohol with browned and overcooked cornbread instead.

Making and selling alcohol had become a somewhat hidden creative activity; Mainers had practice at it, and they had been successful. Dan Herlihy had a successful and lucrative alcohol business enterprise. He was so powerful that people joked that he would never be in jail for violating Prohibition. He lived on Mount Desert Island, and after he was arrested and served about a year in jail, he and his wife went on a six-month-long world-wide cruise. When they returned, they opened Dreamwood, which was noted to have the best dance floor and was the center of entertainment on Mount Desert Island.

There were a number of people spending a great deal of time trying to maneuver around the law. There were private clubs like the one at the Bar Harbor Inn. There were speakeasies all over Bar Harbor and Mount Desert Island for people to socialize in and have a drink. The building that now houses the Bar Harbor Savings and Loan on Main Street in Bar Harbor had a speakeasy in the basement that was designed like a ship and had live music. The Criterion Theater on Cottage Street in Bar Harbor served pickled eggs for a penny and a shot of whiskey for ten cents in the hidden basement area.

Ralph Stanley is a boat builder, among other talents, and he lives on Mount Desert Island. His father was a fisherman. He has been named as a treasure by the Smithsonian. In a talk at the SW Harbor Library on June 30, 2018, Ralph said that the fishing demand was low in the 1920s and '30s, but the fishermen did all right by making booze runs. Many fishermen were part of the lucrative alcohol transportation system during Prohibition. Alcohol came from the Caribbean or Canada according to Ralph.

He told me after the talk that his favorite food was stuffed cusk and cream of tartar biscuits. "It's better than turkey." I had gone to a previous talk by Ralph Stanley and asked him about his favorite food memories of childhood; he had mentioned baked stuffed cusk and cream of tartar biscuits even then. When I asked what the stuffing was made of, he said it was like turkey stuffing. In this world of the internet, there are many types of stuffing, but there is a basic stuffing that shows up in most old cookbooks. In researching stuffing in that period, one would not see the variety of ingredients in a turkey stuffing as there are today. Cusk is not easy to find in stores. It is a mild-tasting fish that is a member of the cod family. The recipe may be found at the end of this chapter.

The end of the Roaring Twenties was followed by the stock market crash of 1929 and then the Great Depression. Downeast Maine was not as severely hit as other more industrial areas. The locals could at least plant their own food and continue a simple life as they had done before. Some of the wealthy were still coming as tourists or getting away from some of the problems in their home areas. People knew their neighbors and helped one another. Several years later, the slowdown in income for farmers and tourism developed, and concerns like taxes began to appear. Lobster prices declined dramatically, as they were considered a luxury. Maine people were independent and used to survival, and some who had been away left their city jobs and moved to return to their birthplace and the ways of rural living. Women, as before, planted food gardens, canned fruits and vegetables and raised chickens and cows. Downeast Maine people are survivors. In the late '30s things were improving in tourism.

How were the Wabanaki people doing? The Wabanaki were moved to reservations and told that they would be taken care of so they didn't need to plant and hunt. They were given white flour and canned foods as well as other foods that the government decided to give them. In a talk on Jordan Pond House grounds, the Abbe Museum had Molly Neptune Parker talk about Wabanaki cooking. She made a soup and fry bread. It was the great combination of no measuring and years of experience. Something she said stood out to me: the Wabanaki spirit of making something from nothing. They are survivors and were determined to make the best of the situation and started cooking with ingredients that did not necessarily make a healthy diet.

When World War II began in the 1940s, Prohibition was over. During the war, Ralph Stanley said, the demand for fish was down, partly because fish was not designated by the United States as an essential food for individuals so there were no ration cards for fish. Lobsters were considered to be a luxury. Meat was rationed, but you could buy all the fish you wanted. Ralph said his father was selling 150 pounds of lobster at fifteen cents a pound. It wasn't until later in the war that fish were recognized, and by then, it was too late for lobstermen to really see a difference. Fishermen were a great asset to the war in that they were the eyes and ears of the country in the pursuit

Planting apple orchards for food and drink. *Author's collection.*

of foreign ships and submarines. The Downeast ship builders constructed vessels for the war effort. Ralph said that one U.S. submarine crew traded their beef, which was apparently rather leathery, to a lobsterman for a large supply of lobster. In the '40s people started eating more mussels, and in 1942, sardine canneries were allowed to be open year-round resulting in an upturn in the market.

Social gatherings often revolve around religious groups and still do today in Downeast Maine. Many cookbooks are from members of religious groups offering their recipes for support of the church. In the Depression, after the fire on Mount Desert Island in 1947, after World War II and during other hard times, Bar Harbor people banded together and looked at ways to economize. A war cake in the *Sanitary Fair Cook Book* (Bangor, 1864), reprinted by the Bangor Historical Society, economized by using no sugar or eggs.

———•———

Recipes

War Cake

Two cups of dried apples cut the size of raisins, soaked in water overnight—in the morning, drain off the water, boil an hour in two cups of molasses—cool it and stir in five cups of flour, one cup of milk, ½ cup of butter, one teaspoonful cloves, one of cinnamon, one of allspice, two teaspoons full soda and one of cream tartar. Add lemon with apples to improve it. Bake one hour or more in one loaf pan.

———•———

It is said that during the Depression, the government gave the marfax bean to Downeast Maine. Canned goods were prominent, and unique recipes for mock pies, seafood loafs and casseroles, with inexpensive desserts like Jell-O, appeared. These were also part of the fad of quick meals from canned or frozen readymade foods that were also available in most areas of the country.

———◆———

Salmon Pea Wiggle

2 tablespoons butter
2 tablespoons flour
1 cup milk
Salt and pepper to taste
1 can peas (or frozen)
1 can salmon

Prepare the cream sauce by heating the butter and flour until combined but not brown. Add milk, salt and pepper and cook until thickened. Add peas and salmon and serve over toast.

• • •

Halibut Loaf

2 cups soft bread crumbs
1 cup cream
1 pound uncooked halibut chopped in small pieces and seasoned with salt and pepper
3 tablespoons minced celery
4 egg whites, beaten

Mix bread crumbs and cream to a paste. Add the rest of the ingredients and cook in a loaf pan at 350 for about 45 minutes. Serve with a tomato sauce.

• • •

Poached Cod with Aioli
Serves 6

3 pounds cod, cut into 6 pieces
2 cups white wine
1 small onion thinly sliced
1 bay leaf
10 whole black peppercorns
2 short fresh thyme sprigs
2 teaspoons salt
6 cups water

Aioli
⅛ teaspoon finely chopped cilantro
1 tablespoon hot water
1 clove garlic, chopped
1 teaspoon finely grated orange zest
¼ cup orange juice
1 tablespoon lemon juice
Salt and pepper to taste
¼ cup or slightly more mayonnaise

Add all of the above but the fish and aioli ingredients to a boil in deep skillet, then reduce heat and simmer 10 minutes. Add fish and simmer for six minutes. Remove skin and serve warm or at room temperature with aioli.

• • •

Haddock with Roasted Red Pepper Sauce
Serves 2

½ cup chopped red peppers
2 tablespoons heavy cream
¼ teaspoon sugar with any water added to desired consistency and then puree the mixture
2 teaspoons lemon juice

1 ½ tablespoons unsalted butter
1 pound haddock
½ each small green, red or yellow peppers julienned
1 tablespoon olive oil

Roast red peppers in oven at 375 degrees until tender, then combine with heavy cream and sugar. Puree to desired texture; water may be added. Heat lemon and butter separately for basting. Broil haddock (about 4 inches from heat), basting with lemon and turning once, 7–10 minutes. Cook peppers in oil. Place sauce on plate, add haddock and sprinkle with peppers.

7

MAINE AS A MAJOR FOOD PRODUCER
FOR AMERICA

Lobster, Seafood, Potatoes and Wild Blueberries
Grow in Demand

Fish on Friday, baked beans on Saturday and leftover baked beans on Sunday morning were Maine traditions. A plan that took the guesswork out of "What shall we have for dinner?" for a few days. Churches, social groups and local organizations had baked bean supper fundraisers. In a discussion with Raymond Strout, a local historian, he remembered his mother sending him to literally pick up dinner. During low tide, on the sand bar going to Bar Island from Bar Harbor, it was possible to pick up flounder and lobsters that got caught up in the tide changes.

One Downeast food problem that may never be resolved completely is that of the baked bean controversy. Baked bean suppers are still very much a part of Maine culture.

It seems that many locals in Downeast Maine have definite opinions about baked beans. There are community suppers and people eager to discuss the correct method of making them. The type of bean itself is controversial. Baked beans grew in popularity, as it is relatively easy and a nutritious meal containing protein. It was popular in lumber camps, church dinners and also as a side dish to hot dogs or other simple foods. I was told that during the Depression that the government sent the marfax (sometimes marifax, marafax) beans to Downeast Maine and they are still considered the best bean by those in Columbia Falls.

Chuck Hammond wrote for the *Coastal Press* before the newspaper owners retired and the paper ended. These are excerpts from his article in 2014:

The Downeast Baked Beans Controversy, Or Spilling the Beans on Downeast Baked Beans

This is perhaps the most controversial subject I have ever written about and I am doing it not withstanding the considerable risk. My wife Roberta and I have attended many bean suppers in and around Columbia Falls. People sit at long tables family style often with friends, neighbors, people you may not know from away. It is an entertaining social event with great conversation, plentiful food and delicious pies. One subject that always comes up is the recipe for baking the Marifax beans; that is whether they should be sweetened or unsweetened. This is not something taken lightly. Downeasters are so passionate about their beans that they can't understand (or won't) the other's point of view. Perhaps nothing is more controversial in Downeast Maine than the recipe for baked beans. Whether you spell it Marfax, Marafax, or Marifax it is the same bean and the only bean served around here. Besides the beans other common ingredients are salt pork, sweetener (molasses, white sugar, brown sugar, or artificial) and onion, but the one ingredient that gets people all worked up is the sweetener or lack of it.

He goes on to say that generally the people north of the tracks, which is now actually a nature walk, liked the beans unsweetened, and those from the south of the old track location like them sweetened. I did speak with his wife, Roberta, and she said that she put molasses in her baked beans and Chuck never complained. At the end of the article, he leaves the reader with this question: "Local historians have always wondered why Columbia and Columbia Falls split back in 1863, do you suppose it was due to the baked bean controversy?"

The controversy over which bean to use and should they be sweetened or unsweetened is prevalent in many areas of Maine. Ruth Eveland at the Jessup Library sent me this essay written by Bill Horner of Bar Harbor. Bill wrote this in advance of a baked bean supper with judging of different baked beans in 2011 on Mount Desert Island:

It is difficult to imagine more closely held opinions than those pertaining to bean selection, pre-cooking preparation, cooking additives and cooking duration. The commonly agreed upon elements of this persistent debate are to start with dried beans, soak overnight, parboil and cook slowly for six or eight hours. Beyond that, it is difficult to find any agreement. Perhaps the liveliest argument starts at the very beginning: which bean should one use?

Lobster roll on table. *Author's collection.*

get out one end. Dip the open end in butter or whatever sauce you like and then take tiny bites from that next joint toward the opening, and the meat will come out.

Lobster can be prepared in many ways, but boiled and eaten with butter is the common way. For those not wanting to get messy, the lobster roll has become popular. A lobster roll is an easy way to get lobster and still not need to clean up afterward. The best lobster roll is the one with the most lobster cut in small pieces and put on a toasted split-side type of hot dog–shaped roll. Maybe one slice of lettuce on the roll before the lobster is added. If you are eating it immediately, you could add melted butter on top. If you will be taking it on a picnic or just like it better, you add a bit of mayonnaise to keep the lobster together. No fillers are necessary but if you really want the crunch of celery, mince the celery and have a bowl that people can add on top. If the lobster roll is served with light bit of mayonnaise, you could still add melted butter if you wanted.

Lobster bisque became popular when lavish dinner parties were more formal, as were lobster croquettes. These were other ways to be lazy and not have all the mess and work of eating a boiled lobster.

WHAT IS THE LIFE span of an industry? Is there a life span for availability of a food?

Industry has changed, companies have changed and our food supply has changed, and it is still changing.

There isn't really a big demand for Maine river block ice any longer. Clothing and shoes are now made in places other than just America. Computers have decreased the need for paper. Shipbuilding has changed course to luxury yachts.

The lobster industry is very important to Downeast Maine. Our biggest worry? Maybe global warming. It is shocking to realize that the Gulf of Maine is one of the fastest-warming bodies of water in the world. Yes, I said the world. The migration of lobsters shows that right now they are here in Downeast Maine, but they are moving north, as areas to the south of us are realizing. One lobsterman in SW Harbor I spoke with said he already saw a decline. Others say that in their area, the temperatures are the same, and they have seen no change in water temperature or in their lobster catch. Studies of water temperature are done on a daily basis. These cold spots that fish and lobster are finding could be attributed to wind and water currents, just as patterns of wind and currents explain where hurricanes go. They help to explain our water patterns. On the West Coast of the United States, there is a town called Sequim, Washington. The Olympic National Park gets 140 to 170 inches of rain a year and is one of the wettest temperate rain forests areas in the contiguous United States. Sequim is a town on the road to the Olympia rainforest from Portland, Oregon. It is in an arid patch of land with less than sixteen inches of rain each year. This strange anemology is because of the way the wind currents happen to come to it. Are there parts of the Downeast coast that will not be affected by global warming because of the way the winds and currents make their way up the coast? Lobster will find some cold spots for a while. Cod may find those spots that are cold for a while as well.

Currently we are doing OK as far as the numbers of lobster caught and sold. The lobstermen seem to feel that the lobster catch is being well managed. Many worry that we are at a point that we could see a sharp decline. The lower coast of the Gulf of Maine has seen a devastating effect in ocean-related foods over the past ten to twenty years. Downeast lobsters and fish have been migrating north for colder waters. Research is being done by many scientists and organizations with the hope of finding an answer.

Researchers have found that larger/older lobster females can produce more eggs than smaller, younger ones. A lot more. According to Mark

Kurlansky, cod also follow this pattern. In the book *Cod: A Biography of the Fish that Changed the World*, Kurlansky states a female cod that is forty inches long could produce three million eggs in a spawning. The larger cod of fifty inches could produce nine million eggs. The eggs create a film on the water and are threatened by rough water and by being sought after by other species looking for food. Most don't survive, but if young cod do survive, they can live up to thirty years. Mark Kurlanski makes an interesting comment about seeing something that doesn't work but not going back to the way it did work. He said, "But technology never reverses itself. It creates a new technology to confront new sets of problems."

Whose territory is it to fish? How much is too much for a haul? What restrictions are good for the resurgence of the fish but don't hurt fisherman? Global warming is here, and fishermen realize it. Should they catch all the fish they can now before they migrate north? Should they study and keep fish repopulating with hope the fish can adapt to the changing warmer conditions? There are no easy answers.

As ships changed, so did fishing. The sailing boats gave way to steam-powered boats and then diesel-powered boats, enabling fishermen to chase

Water sources were plentiful. *Author's collection.*

the fish. Now boats were catching more fish, and competition was growing to get the fish and then bring them to market first. Too many fish could cause the market to crash. A good season is usually not a bad thing, but they can cause problems. The biggest concerns are to get the fish to market fresh and to have waiting buyers. Keeping fish fresh is and was the key. Salted fish gave way to the new frozen foods. Many fish manufacturing success stories followed. *Fresh frozen* became a new term.

Haddock is the Maine fish that is most common here. It is low in mercury, readily available and is good for many recipes, as it is a mild whitefish. You will probably find haddock on most menus in Downeast.

Atlantic salmon is the Maine state fish. Currently there is no commercial fishing for the Atlantic salmon or for our Maine shrimp. In 2000, the United States listed the Atlantic salmon as an endangered species. The decline was because of a number of factors, including pollution, global warming, overfishing and habitat disturbance by straightening rivers and not leaving the little habitats they prefer. The Department of Marine Resources released 100,000 smolts in 2016, hoping that the salmon will adapt and return to rivers like the Narraguagus. The Narragaugus used to be a center of fly-fishing for salmon.

Cooking fish is the art of not letting it cook too long. Fish should be cooked until it is just flaky. There are a number of fish other than haddock, such as hake, cusk and mackerel, in Downeast, but you don't see them as often because haddock and cod are available in larger quantities right now or other fish is not as much in demand.

Fishing in Maine is suffering from the effects of global warming. Fish want to be in an area that works for them just as people live in areas that make sense to them for whatever reason. Fish and lobster in Downeast like cold water. The Gulf of Maine is one of several of the most rapidly warming bodies of water in the world. Fish and lobster have been migrating north to colder waters for years. In the migration charts, 2018 lobster looked alright for Downeast Maine, unlike some areas farther south in the Gulf of Maine. There are many studies and concerns in this area, and factual information is available that shows the effects of global warming.

What happened to our Maine shrimp? They were small and sweet and were good for many recipes. It wasn't that they were the biggest shrimp, but their taste was one of the top.

Our Maine shrimp have largely disappeared. We no longer have a shrimp industry. Why? Many reasons lead primarily to global warming. Often, sea temperatures trigger mating, when to spawn and other aspects of their life in the sea. The Maine shrimp doesn't fit the typical "the bigger the better" American philosophy. So, you might not be happy to get them in a shrimp cocktail. Gulf of Maine shrimp are great in chowder and many other dishes because of their flavor; that can easily be eaten by fork or spoon. It was a hard financial blow to fishermen who fished for shrimp during the winter season. The shrimp season fit in between other sources of fishing income. The shrimp population has not returned from the closing of the industry in 2014, as the warming water is not hospitable to recovery. A few restaurants have been carrying Canadian shrimp from the Gulf of Maine, but even some of those restaurants have switched over to the cheaper shrimp from Malaysia, Indonesia and now India.

Sardines were fashionable to eat at one time, but they don't appear too often anymore. Sardine factories were too smelly for tourists' and homeowners' comfort, and they slowly disappeared. Sardines are important in our circle of life here. Every time we lose/replace a species, there are many other ripples that occur. The sardines are essential for bait in the lobster industry. It is sometimes difficult to see the big picture. Without the very small fish, many species are in jeopardy. Birds are a good example. There are cute little children's books about puffins and stuffed puffins that tourists buy without knowing the other side of global warming and climate change. Without small fish like the sardines, real puffins are unable to feed their young. Puffins can't find small enough fish to feed their young, so the babies choke to death on fish that are too large or starve. Sardines also are essential to the lobster industry. Lobsters like herring and so do cod.

In 2017, Sarah Madronal, Downeast Salmon Federation biologist, gave a talk at the Southwest Harbor library about herring. Our blueback herring is the same species all up and down the East Coast to Florida. The herring were caught in weirs, and there is extensive use of herring as bait for lobster and halibut. Jonesport is a part of the Downeast history with river herring. The Passamaquoddy waters and fish have always been a part of their history. A plain herring is called a sardine. River herring are used mostly for bait. Herring are not as large an industry due to depletion, so the costs are expected to rise. There were regulations adopted in the middle of the 2018 season that cut the quota from 110,000 to about 50,000 metric tons. Madronal said that in the 1700s, there was a rule that gave each widow a barrel of alewives.

Wild blueberries are a very important crop in Maine for their taste and for our health. Cherryfield, Maine, claims to be the world's capital of wild blueberries, and Downeast Maine is the world's largest producer of wild blueberries. This is indicated on an old sign that you see as you travel on

Route 1 coming into town. Cherryfield is on the Narraguas River. In the summer, when the salmon were running, the town had daily competitions, with a posting of the biggest catch of the day and cash prizes awarded. The salmon are no longer there, but residents are trying to clean up the river and bring them back. Evidently, overboard discharge is one of the lingering problems along with warming waters. There are eighty-one homes in Cherryfield in the National Register of Historic Places.

Downeast Maine is the largest producer of wild blueberries, and it is the hope of Downeast Mainers that it will remain that way. What could be happier than wild blueberries? What could do so much for your health while giving you a delicious taste that can be used in so many recipes? Blueberries are now known for the super food that they are. They are packed with vitamins, and because of their small size, a cup of wild blueberries is twice as nutritious as cultivated blueberries. Macias has an annual Blueberry Festival, and I had an opportunity to talk with a number of people when asked to be a judge for the blueberry cooking contest. It was a fun occasion, with a musical about blueberry harvesting put on by practically everyone in the town both old and young.

Downeast Maine, world's largest producer of wild blueberries. *Author's collection.*

Salmon fishing tournaments with prizes each day. *Author's collection.*

Organic wild blueberry farm stand, Cherryfield, Maine. *Author's collection.*

Cross roads on Main Street and Route 1 in Cherryfield, Maine. *Author's collection.*

So, how could the blueberry farmers be unhappy? Life never seems to be easy. Let me start by explaining that there are many blueberry fields in Downeast Maine. Most of the fields work with a company that sells fresh blueberries for the farmer or freezes the blueberries to sell and ship year-round. Canada can process them cheaper than the United States, so companies have been investing in blueberry fields and processing blueberries in Canada and even processing some of the wild blueberries in other states. In 2018, the processing companies gave the farmers a price that many farmers found too low to get help, fertilize, weed and so forth and still make any profit. Many decided to leave the fields and just not harvest at all. So, there are no wild blueberries, you say? Well, the companies don't really need Maine blueberries as much, since Canada can produce them with less expense to the corporations. Blueberry company headquarters are moving away from the Maine fields. Bottom line or years of tradition? The answer seems to be leaning toward bottom line.

The *Quoddy Tides* considers itself the most easterly newspaper published in the United States. In the August 11, 2017 issue, there was a front-page article that sums up some of the problems in the blueberry industry. In the newspaper's interview with Justin Day, eighty-one, Day explains that ten years ago, farmers were receiving one dollar a pound for blueberries. In 2017, they were offered fifteen cents a pound. He stressed that he couldn't hire people and care for and raise and rake blueberries for that amount. He didn't plan to rake his fields. He, after his family had the blueberry fields since 1900, didn't see a future in blueberries. Another grower also noted that he had also heard of farmers not harvesting because of the uncertainty of price but also not enough bees for pollination and damp weather causing blossom blight. The blueberry raking community has a communal connection and a social aspect to it. Also featured in the article, Matt Dana of Indian Township has been raking on the tribe's land since he was twelve and has gone each year for twenty years. Now, he takes his family with three children to the annual blueberry raking. It is community and families sharing food, cooking together and playing games in the evening.

The American Potato Association says types of potatoes include white, red, russet, blue and yellow, and over two hundred kinds are grown in America. Potatoes are easy to grow in our soil and climate in Maine. Maine is the largest producer of potatoes in the country. No, we aren't. We were number one. Yes, we were, but we are no longer number one. That's true. Maine was the largest producer of potatoes in the 1930s and '40s, but people started moving west and planted potatoes in places like Idaho and California. In 2018, Maine ranked about fourteenth in production of potatoes in the United States. The potato industry flourished in the early years but now is trying to find a niche in a declining demand, except for french fry and potato chip companies.

We are talking about the 1700 and 1800s, when this new crop had evolved. You could make a lot of meals based around a potato, and it has B6, vitamin C, magnesium, potassium, and half of amount of recommended daily fiber is in the skin. It certainly was helpful for supplying food for the new communities. It did well in Maine and became a versatile ingredient in many recipes.

The potato industry is trying to find its way into niche markets with new potato strains/types. When people began migrating West, they started planting potatoes, corn and grain. Trains were available for transportation, and our potato industry started slipping from first place.

Potatoes are good for many recipes and as substitutes in cooking. You could use a quarter cup of mashed potatoes as a substitute for an egg. A very popular candy in Maine called Needhams were made with mashed potatoes.

Our white potato is also great for chowders because it holds up well when cooked in water. However, most of the potatoes in Maine today are now sold to manufacturers for fries or potato chips. They are valued for their thin skins, which make it unnecessary to peel the potato first.

In an interview on NPR's *All Things Considered* regarding the potato industry, Senator Susan Collins said she grew up and picked potatoes in Aroostook County. Baked stuffed potato with cheese is the senator's favorite potato dish. She said, "Looks good on a plate and can't be beat."

———•———

RECIPES

Crab Cake

½ pound crabmeat
1 egg
2–3 tablespoons capers
Cracker crumbs like saltines or chowder crackers

Mix all ingredients except crackers. Pat into small patty and cover in crumbs. Fry in organic sunflower oil until golden brown.

• • •

Scallops

One of my favorite ways to prepare scallops is to cook them at medium heat in butter. Remove them from the pan when cooked to a solid white throughout and then add Grand Marnier to the hot pan. Add cream and then pour over scallops.

• • •

Sardines on Toast

Place drained canned sardines on toast. Spread with a spicy mustard and broil until hot. Eat while warm. Good for an appetizer, snack or lunch.

• • •

Baked Beans From Away

1 pound marfax/marafax/marifax beans soaked in water overnight
1 tablespoon dry mustard
2 tablespoons brown sugar
1 cup water
2 tablespoons molasses
½ pound salt pork cut on the diagonal (or ⅓ cup oil, but it is better with salt pork)
1 medium white onion
1 organic apple, halved and cored

Dissolve mustard and sugar in a cup of water. Drain beans and put in above ingredients except apple and cover with fresh water, pork placed on top.

Bring to boil, then put in oven at 300 for 5 hours, leaving the top off for last hour. Add apple to the pot during the last hour.

• • •

Banana and Blueberry Sorbet
A Too Easy Dessert

Everyone has leftover bananas, and I know some get thrown away. Everyone is not making smoothies or baking banana bread every day. So here is another thought.

1 banana
1 ½ cups or so frozen wild blueberries

Put them together in a food processor, and a few minutes later, you can be serving a healthy light dessert.

• • •

Blueberry Molded Dessert

Another incredibly easy desert with little preparation. It just has to sit awhile.

Use a bowl or form that can serve as a mold. Cut the crusts off sliced bread and layer them in the mold so that they just overlap and none of the mold is showing. Have enough wild blueberries to fill the bowl; add ¼ cup to ½ cup sugar to them if needed. Place the berries in the mold and add a weight to push the mixture down. An inverted plate with a can on top would work. Place in the refrigerator for about six hours or overnight. Invert the mold onto a serving plate and serve. Whipped cream is an option for serving. The bread will have turned blue.

• • •

Banana Waffles with a Pecan Maple Syrup

Syrup
1 cup maple syrup
½ cup pecans, roasted and coarsely chopped
4 tablespoons lemon juice or orange juice

⅔ cup white rice flour
½ cup cornmeal
2 tablespoons sugar
4 teaspoons baking powder
½ teaspoon salt
2 bananas
⅔ cup water
4 eggs
4 tablespoons unsalted butter, melted and cool
Safflower/sunflower oil, for brushing waffle pan, if needed

Bring syrup and pecans to a boil, add juice and keep warm. Whisk dry ingredients. Puree bananas and water, and in another bowl add eggs and butter. Incorporate dry ingredients. Keep warm in 200-degree oven, makes four waffles.

• • •

Oeuf & Jambon en Cassolette

This is an easy brunch recipe with very little effort.

Shaved ham
1 hard-boiled egg, chopped
Crème fraîche or heavy cream

Heat until hot, about 5 minutes at 400 degrees.

Vegetarian Version

Blanched spinach
1 hard-boiled egg chopped
Crème fraîche or heavy cream
Gruyere sprinkled on top if desired

Heat until hot, about 5 minutes at 400 degrees.

• • •

Potatoes Anna

Thinly sliced potatoes
Butter
Salt and pepper to taste

Have enough potatoes to fit into a mold or several small individual molds. In a circular pattern, overlapping, brush each layer starting on the bottom of the mold with butter. Place in oven at 375 until potatoes are tender. To serve, invert mold and serve.

8

SUMMER FOODS AND SUMMER PEOPLE

You have heard of them. Maybe wondered how the rich and famous lived and what they ate. I would guess they all had lobster at some point during their stay in Downeast, but our other crops and small gardens lend themselves to memorable settings with a warm summer breeze, stars lighting up the black night skies and seasonal foods.

Presidents, dignitaries, the famous and wealthy have been on Mount Desert Island and many have built or purchased homes here. They had staff, and they entertained. Lobster has been a special dish for many years.

It is said that John D. Rockefeller liked meat and potatoes, but toward the end of his life, his diet was 75 percent fruit and vegetables. He didn't drink alcohol. David Rockefeller Sr. remembered great juices being served at his father's many dinner parties, but alcohol was never offered, according to an interview for the MDI Historical Society. President Wilson dedicated Acadia National Park. His doctor and staff were concerned that he was too thin and wasn't very interested in food. They did a survey of his staff, and it was noted he seemed to like chicken salad for lunch.

Henry Ford ate mostly soy products. President Barack Obama and Michelle had a date night while visiting Bar Harbor in 2010. She had Lobster Thermidor; he had paella.

Julia Child spent many summers in Bernard on Mount Desert Island. Julia McWilliams came to the Mount Desert Island with Paul Child to meet her future family in the early 1950s, and they continued coming there until she died. She and Paul stayed at the family compound on Lopaus Point, or Old

Beautiful vistas. *Author's collection.*

Landscapes of luxury waterfront estates. *Author's collection.*

Right: Julia Child. *Photograph by Paul Child Schlesinger Library, Radcliffe Institute, Harvard University Image 405223.*

Below: Julia Child's cat Copper trying to reap the rewards from the day's catch. *Photograph by Paul Child Schlesinger Library, Radcliffe Institute, Harvard University Image 586860.*

Point as they use to call it. The Child family built the house and additions with logs they cut, prepared and moved and constructed over the years. Julia learned a bit of carpentry during that period. There is a nice book by Paul's twin brother, Charles, that spoke about building the home on Lopaus Point in Bernard on Mount Desert Island over a number of years. It was a diary of many family building projects at the Maine house, including taking down trees and using the logs to make additions. The family seemed to live a simple life while here. At some point, Charles started planning a new wing. The family was growing, and there was a possibility of getting power from bottled gas. Charles got the planning started: "Yes, of course, bigger windows; the view to the sea on the southwest corner side was superb now that the forest had been thinned out. And that delicious new kitchen, everything planned so that food would positively flow from bins to stove to table."

The brainstorming blossomed, and they caught fish and clams and ate other seafood. There was a suggestion made that the kitchen they were going to create should have a special small fireplace inside the kitchen at table height to grill steaks, as they all loved steaks.

He talks about how excited Paul and Julia were and eager to help. Julia and the other women were given the job of scraping the bark from the trees plus other carpentry duties.

Later in the book, Charles Child talks about Julia and Paul getting back from being stationed in France. They were planning to spend a few weeks with the family in Bernard, and Julia had just graduated from Le Cordon Bleu in Paris:

Now a full-fledged and skilled exponent of la haute cuisine, she immediately took Erica and Rachel under her wing and began to give them lessons in high-style French cooking. The consumption of chocolate, butter, wine, mushrooms and egg yolks went up by leaps and bounds as the kitchen of Great Hall became the center of vast activity. Poulet de Breese a la mode de Nantua, Lobster Archduke, lovely little cakes, moules marinara, bouillabaisse, sauce Béarnaise, flowed out in a never-ending stream. And I let my belt out another notch!

Julia and Paul spent many quiet summers on the water. The family still has the hand-built home there. The small fireplace for grilling steaks was added. It wasn't unusual to see Julia Child on the island over the years. She liked cats and had cats named Pewter and Copper. Copper obviously appreciated the fish that the family caught.

Enjoying the afternoon with a friend having lobsters. *Author's collection.*

Glamour, or simplicity of Maine's favorite food, lobster, attracts tourists to come to Downeast. People who have visited and will visit will seek out this famous food.

RECIPES

Understanding seasons is a way of life for some and a wish to live by the seasons for others. Maine seasons vary depending on the year. If it is a warm year, seasons will start earlier and last longer. If it is a cold year, seasons will start later and end earlier. There are many islands along the coast of Downeast Maine. Their location has an effect on the temperature. Islands are usually warmer than inland areas in the winter and cooler than inland areas of Maine in the summer, which makes the coast of Maine a refreshing change for those having very high temperatures in some southern states. The seasons of Downeast Maine provide an opportunity to grow a garden or visit one of the many farmer's markets. Year-round locals and visitors have an opportunity to feast on fresh food. You don't need a lot of room to start a garden.

MARCH

Maple Syrup

A wonderful dessert that will fool most guests is if you use just a little maple syrup drizzled over a good vanilla ice cream. You will be happy you tried it and will have it on hand for this dessert besides pancakes and waffles. To make maple butter for popovers or other breads, cream butter and maple syrup to taste.

Maple syrup Sunday at the Nutkin Knoll one-hundred-acre farm. *Author's collection.*

APRIL/MAY

Fiddleheads

Fiddleheads are an ostrich fern that is found out in wet areas in the woods. They are cut when they are about six to eight inches tall and have not filled out as a fern. Use ostrich ferns, as other ferns may be poisonous. You are now seeing fiddleheads in many high-end grocery stores, but they grow in cold climates. We know it is fiddlehead season when a guy with a truck is on the side of the road with a sign that says "fiddleheads." They should be rinsed and then either boiled or steamed to rid them of any toxins. After boiling them for ten minutes, they should then be quickly put on ice or in cold water so they don't continue to cook and get mushy. They can then be used in any manner after that initial preparation in any way you might prepare asparagus. They taste like asparagus and can be sautéed in butter, made into a quiche or an omelet or added to a variety of other dishes.

June

Dandelions, Spinach, Continuation of Radishes, Peas, Mint, Lettuce, Carrots, Asparagus

You can tell summer is here with the first appearance of a number of foods. Dandelions, if not sprayed by weed killer, can be eaten in their entirety. The leaves should be picked before the flower blossoms, as they are most tender then. The flowers have a mild taste and make a nice addition to a salad, or you could try making wine from it. The roots can be dried and ground into a coffee.

Maine Dandelions with Salt Pork and Potatoes

Cook about ½ pound of salt pork in water to just cover it. At medium heat, it should start to steam. Turn the heat down and cook slowly for about an hour. Then add greens and potatoes that have been pared and cook until potatoes are tender, maybe a half hour or so.

July

Strawberries, Summer Squash, Tomatoes, Zucchini, Peas, Mint, Lettuce, Chives, Swiss Chard, Broccoli, Asparagus, Beets, Basil

Tomato Sauce

2 onions
½ cup organic olive oil
6 ounces tomato paste
4 pounds organic tomatoes, cleaned and chopped
¼ cup basil
¼ cup oregano
4 cloves garlic, cut in half

Sauté onions in olive oil until tender. Add other ingredients and simmer for thirty to forty minutes. Let cool if keeping some for freezing. It freezes well.

• • •

Country Fried Tomatoes

1 teaspoon sugar
½ cup flour
½ teaspoon salt
¼ teaspoon pepper
6 medium green tomatoes
½ cup butter

Mix dry ingredients and coat the tomatoes with the mixture. Fry at medium temperature in butter or ½ butter and half organic sunflower oil. Serve as crisp or add ½ cup cream and pour over tomatoes.

• • •

Zucchini-Watercress Soup

2 cups chopped yellow onions
4 tablespoons butter
3 cups chicken stock
2 pounds zucchini, cut bite-size pieces

1 bunch watercress
Lemon to taste, 1 teaspoon or more

Sauté onions in butter. Add stock, zucchini and watercress after onion has cooked and cook until zucchini is tender.

• • •

Cream of Zucchini Soup

3 cups zucchini, sliced
½ cup water
1 tablespoon minced onion
2 tablespoon butter
2 tablespoon flour
½ teaspoon seasoned salt
½ cup chicken stock
½ cup milk
¾ cup light cream
Sour cream, for garnish

In a saucepan, stir all but milk and cream until blended and then add the milk and cream. Serve with a topping of a spoon of sour cream.

• • •

Zucchini Fans

Zucchini
Cherry tomatoes
Basil
Olive Oil
Mozzarella
Parmesan

Cut zucchini horizontally into about 4-inch pieces. Turn them on their end and make about three cuts down about an inch and a half. In the slices put a small slice of cherry tomato sprinkled with basil. Heat oven to 400 degrees. Coat pan with olive oil and add fans; drizzle oil over and cook twenty-five minutes.

Place in squares of mozzarella, sprinkle with parmesan and heat at 475 until melted.

AUGUST

Wild Maine Blueberries, Spinach, Watermelon, Sweet Peppers, Onions, Green Beans, Garlic, Cucumbers, Corn, Cantaloupes, Blackberries, Apples Now through October

Machias, Maine Blueberry Festival contest finalists. *Author's collection.*

Glazed Blueberry Muffins

½ cup soft butter
1 cup sugar
2 large eggs
¾ to 1 cup milk, as needed
2 teaspoons baking powder
1 teaspoon baking soda
2 cups flour
1 teaspoon vanilla extract
Zest of 1 lemon
1–2 cups wild blueberries

Cream butter and sugar. Add eggs one at a time and then milk. Add this to dry ingredients. Incorporate vanilla, zest and berries. Bake at 350 for about 20–25 minutes.

Glaze
Lemon juice
Confectioner's sugar

Add fresh lemon juice to about ¾ cup sugar until you have a consistency that will just pour in a thick stream.

September

String Beans, Colored Carrots, Cauliflower, Brussels Sprouts, Turnips, Winter Squash, Grapes

Chickpea Dip with Garlic and Cumin

2½ cups chickpea (garbanzo bean)
1 small clove garlic
3 tablespoons olive oil
2 teaspoons fresh lemon juice, or to taste

1 teaspoon cumin
2 tablespoons tahini
1 medium roasted carrot (could microwave until tender)

Puree and thin if needed with more olive oil.

• • •

Tapenade

½ cup black kalamata olives
¼ cup green olives
2 anchovy filets
1 clove garlic
2 tablespoons oil-packed tuna, drained
2 tablespoons drained capers
1 tablespoon lemon juice
1 cup fresh basil
¼ cup olive oil

Process all in a food processor. While blending, dribble in olive oil. For a dip, add mayonnaise. Fill tomatoes, grilled eggplants, bread or other possibilities.

OCTOBER

Squash, Pumpkins, Potatoes, Eggplant, Parsnips, Cranberries

OCTOBER/NOVEMBER

Wild Cranberries, Continuation of Potatoes, Brussels Sprouts, Cauliflower, Leeks, Lettuce, Parsnips, Winter Squash

Seasons changing into fall. *Author's collection*.

Eggplant and Potato au Gratin

1 cup cubed white potato
1 cup cubed eggplant
Vegetable stock
Salt
Pepper
1 egg yolk
1 teaspoon tomato paste
Cream, up to ⅓ cup, if needed
Mozzarella

Cook the potato and eggplant together in vegetable stock until tender. Drain the stock. Put the eggplant and potato in a food processor. Add a little salt and pepper and egg yolk. Puree with a little tomato paste for color and add cream that is enough to make a thick batter consistency. Place in an ovenproof container. Add strips of mozzarella on top. Cook at 350 for about 25 minutes.

• • •

Roasted Vegetables with Rosemary

½ cup olive oil
1 pound eggplant cut crosswise into ½-inch pieces
4 large plum tomatoes cut lengthwise into ½-inch slices
Onion, cut into ½-inch slices
Zucchini in lengthwise pieces to fit
Red potato, cut into ½-inch slices
½ pound mozzarella cut into (6) ¼-inch slices
½ cup of ricotta, with 2 teaspoon thyme, ½ teaspoon ground rosemary, salt and pepper
6 fresh rosemary twigs

Roast all the vegetables on a baking sheet with a little olive oil on pan for about 20 minutes or until tender. Let cool.

Layer vegetables with a slice of mozzarella on top and ricotta mixture between vegetables to hold them together. Use rosemary to keep the vegetables together by skewering from the top in each bundle. Adjust recipe for the number of people and if you would use it as an appetizer, side dish or main course. Cook at 450 with little olive oil, about 10–15 minutes

Tip: Do batch cooking to roast more vegetables than you need for this dish so they can be easily fit into more meals.

• • •

Artichokes with Parmesan

2 minced cloves garlic
⅓ cup Parmesan cheese
⅓ cup bread crumbs
⅓ cup raisins
2 artichokes, clean in lemon juice and clip ends
Organic olive oil, for drizzle

Mix filling ingredients. Stuff artichokes and drizzle olive oil over chokes. Bake about an hour at 350.

Note: I will sometimes microwave the artichoke for two minutes first so that the cooking time is less, and either way you can test it for being done by tugging on one of the leaves. If it comes off easily, it is done.

• • •

Artichoke with Melted Butter

This way of cooking artichokes is to clean the artichoke in a bowl of water with a little vinegar added. That will kill bacteria and cleans other vegetables. Then, immediately rinse it in a colander.

Clip ends of leaves and boil in a pot for about twenty minutes or until a leaf come off easily. Dip leaves into melted butter and enjoy.

• • •

Cold Stuffed Artichoke with Shrimp and Remoulade

Prepare artichoke as described above. Let the artichoke cool, and it can be used for any type of cold stuffing or sauce. Gulf of Maine shrimp are best for this, but since Maine no longer has a shrimp industry, you might be able to get them from Canada.

Small cooked shrimp is stuffed between leaves, and remoulade is drizzled over it, with more sauce reserved for dipping.

Remoulade
1 cup mayonnaise
1 ½ tablespoons mustard
4 ounces gherkins
2 ounces capers
1 tablespoon each chopped parsley, chervil and tarragon
½ tablespoon mashed anchovy

Combine an hour before serving and refrigerate.

• • •

Goat Cheese, Tomato and Basil Salad

5 tomatoes, sliced and cut in half
1 medium purple onion, cut into thin rings
Fresh basil with a little olive oil, pureed (¼ cup)
¼ cup chopped black olives
Salad turnips for crunch
1 tablespoon parsley
¼ cup olive oil
Dash of red vinegar
Salt and pepper
Goat cheese

Combine all ingredients, with goat cheese sprinkled over top.

• • •

Squash Fritters

1 pint sifted squash
1 quart milk
3 eggs
1 teaspoon baking soda
Salt to taste
Flour

Mix all and add enough flour to stiffen batter. Fry in organic sunflower oil.

Lobster is caught year-round, and crabs usually have more meat in them in the fall. When you are able to get fresh seafood year-round, you become more adept at trying new ways of cooking it.

Lobster is usually boiled in Downeast Maine. A lobster pound is where the lobster is kept live until it is bought and cooked. Lobster is caught all year, but there are strict guidelines as to which can be kept. A lobster is measured from the eye socket to the beginning

What an easy way to enjoy lobster. A lobster roll on a beautiful summer day on an outside porch. *Author's collection.*

of the tail. If it is smaller than 3¼ inches, it must be thrown back. If it is larger than 5 inches when measured, it must be thrown back. Female lobsters carrying eggs must also be thrown back after the tail has been notched to indicate she may not legally be caught. When cooking a 1¼- or 1½-pound lobster, it should take around 12 to 15 minutes. The lobster will be red and tail curved under.

• • •

Homard à la Français

Sauce
5 large tomatoes peeled, seeded and chopped (about 3 cups)
¼ cup finely chopped scallions
¼ cup finely chopped carrots
½ cup finely chopped onions
Butter
Fresh parsley
Fresh thyme
Fresh bay leaf
1 cup dry white wine
1 cup chicken or vegetable stock
1 tablespoon tomato past

1 tablespoon flour
½ lemon juice
1 tablespoon finely chopped fresh tarragon
Salt and pepper

2 lobsters
6 tablespoons olive oil
⅓ cup cognac

Sauté vegetables in butter until soft, take off heat and add finely chopped fresh parsley, thyme and bay leaf. Incorporate all remaining sauce ingredients. Remove bay leaf from completed sauce. Cook lobster in boiling water for about 12 to 15 minutes for 1¼-pound lobster. Cool and cut tail into large pieces. On high heat, cook lobster and shell pieces in oil, then quickly pour off all but a film under lobster. Warm cognac and add over lobster. This more modern approach combines the vegetables, sauce and lobster.

December/January

Gulf of Maine Shrimp (no longer)

Spice-Curried Mussels

2 shallots, finely chopped
1 tablespoon unsalted butter
1¼ teaspoons curry
¼ teaspoon hot pepper flakes
¼–½ cup water
3 tablespoons sherry
1 pound mussels
½ cup heavy cream
2 tablespoons chopped cilantro

Sauté shallots in butter and add curry, pepper flakes, water and sherry. Clean mussels and discard any that are open. Bring to a boil and add mussels. Mussels are done when shells open. Discard any mussels that do not open. Remove mussels and add cream and cilantro to broth for dipping.

• • •

Rolled Haddock with Egg Sauce

6 strips of haddock fillet, about a pound and a half, or three large pieces, cut in half lengthwise
A little melted butter
1 ½ cups soft bread crumbs
2 tablespoons minced onion
2 tablespoons minced parsley
Salt and pepper

Spread ingredients over fish and roll them lengthwise. Place on baking sheet with parchment and bake at 350 for about 10 minutes or until flaky.

Egg Sauce
2 tablespoons butter
2 tablespoons flour
1 cup milk
1 hard-boiled egg, chopped

Cook butter and flour, add milk and heat until thick and add egg.

• • •

Halibut Poached in Beer with Red Onion Sauce

1 small carrot, finely chopped
1 celery stalk, finely chopped
2 bay leaves

1 teaspoon black peppercorns
1 cup fish or vegetable stock
1 (12-ounce) bottle pale beer
4 7–8 ounce halibut steaks

Sauce
Reserved liquid
2 small red onions, finely chopped
4 tablespoon butter

Bring all but the halibut to a boil, add fish and reduce to low, covered for about 5 minutes, and remove from heat. Remove 1 cup of poaching liquid, cover fish and let rest 10 minutes. Test to see if fish is flaky.

For sauce, bring liquid in pan to a boil, reduce heat to medium, add onion and reduce by $2/3$, remove from heat and whisk in the butter. Drain fish and serve sauce on the side.

• • •

Baked Cod Steaks with Spinach and Feta

1 pound spinach
¼ cup chopped white scallion
1 tablespoon olive oil
1 clove garlic, minced
2 tablespoons chopped Kalamata olives
½ teaspoon dried oregano
½ cup crumbled feta
1 tablespoon lemon juice
4 pieces cod (about 2 pounds)

Cook spinach and chop. In skillet, sauté scallion until soft and add garlic. Stir in the rest, except fish. Arrange cod on slightly oiled baking dish. Top with mixture and bake at 450 degrees for 8–10 minutes.

• • •

Halibut or Cod with Olive Tarragon Bread Crumbs on Roasted Tomato Platform

¾ pound plum tomatoes (about 6, cut into ¼ inch slices)
4 cloves garlic, unpeeled
½ cup balsamic vinegar
2 6–8 ounce pieces of fish
1 tablespoon mayonnaise
½ teaspoon Dijon mustard
½ cup fresh breadcrumbs
1 ½ tablespoons finely chopped fresh tarragon leaves
2½ tablespoons chopped Kalamata olives
2 tablespoons extra-virgin olive oil, plus 1 tablespoon for brushing pan

Roast tomatoes and garlic coated in balsamic in a 450-degree oven until lightly brown and garlic soft. Puree. Place fish on top of tomato platform. Mix mayonnaise and mustard and coat fish. Pat on breadcrumbs, add tarragon and olives. Drizzle with 2 tablespoons olive oil.

Cook at 450 degrees for 8–10 minutes.

• • •

Cod in Parchment

2 4-ounce cod filets
2 15-inch squares cooking parchment
1 large red pepper, charred
4 thin slices bacon, cut crosswise into thin strips
1 medium Idaho potato, peeled and cut into ½-inch pieces
1 cup chopped onion
1 teaspoon minced garlic
4 scallions, sliced
Salt and pepper
2 tablespoons unsalted butter, melted
2 teaspoons olive oil

Heat oven to 425. Place fish on top of parchment paper, cook all ingredients 15 minutes in packets and then serve with an X in the top of packet.

• • •

Irish Coffee Ice

Strong coffee
Brown sugar to taste, 1 to 2 teaspoons
Irish whiskey, 1 ½ ounces per cup
Heavy cream

Freeze 8 hours, whisking often. Have this on hand for a special dessert.

9
TODAY'S FOOD IN DOWNEAST

Tourists Are Coming by Car, Train and Cruise Ship

What is now, and what is next? Maine is selling lobsters throughout the country and also exporting them to Europe and Asia. We are seeing the harvesting of other delicacies besides lobster for export to foreign markets. Small companies are working with seaweed, kelp, worms and eels to sell to Asia. Our grocery stores are trying to fill the most need in the food supply. It would not make sense for a grocery store to buy a few items that people might not buy or even want. However, people might prefer items that the large chain stores don't make as much profit from. Grocery stores, as any industry, need to sell products from which they will gain the most profit. Seasons for foods are blurred by the imports from many countries in the world. Someone, somewhere, is growing foods that we want at any time of the year. Also, frozen foods and canned goods fill in gaps when fresh foods are not available. Unless you grow your own food or eat seasonally through a farmer's market or organic health food store, your food intake is determined by the choices that a grocery chain makes. The internet is trying to get in on this by having an even larger selection of foods and spices to compete with the grocery chains, and the quantities they buy can lower the price even more. Will the chain grocery stores continue to thrive with giving the consumer the traditional limited selection? We are becoming more educated in our choices. The internet can explain the chemicals and additives added to help preserve foods. Information on nutrition may be found.

Do we have time to stop and think about our meals in our busy lives? How can we make the most of what we have? How can we plan so that

Tourists come by plane. *Author's collection.*

Tourists visit on cruise ships and arrive at the town pier by tender. *Author's collection.*

when we buy food there is less waste? We are learning about and using good organic foods and understanding how they help our health. Maine organic blueberries should be in everyone's freezer, yet many people don't realize that a cup of wild blueberries has twice the nutritional benefits as a cup of cultivated blueberries.

Are we headed toward growing our own organic gardens and seeing the reduction of waste and increase in better foods, or are we going to start another industry to fix the problems we have in foods?

We, as Americans, want things that are quick, easy, that taste good, that are impressive and healthy. We want everything.

Industries have come and gone. It is good to realize that things change. But we don't want to see some of the possible changes in our food resources due to global warming. Thankfully, there are researchers studying how to prevent a loss of our seafood resources. Remember the Gulf of Maine is one of the fastest-warming bodies of water in the world due to global warming.

Lobster, blueberries, seafood and the beautiful coast of Downeast Maine bring millions of people here each year. It is a wonderful place to appreciate, as many magazines and travel programs will confirm.

The wild blueberry farmers have concerns that even though Hancock and Washington Counties in Maine are the largest producers of wild blueberries in the world, companies are planting and/or processing wild blueberries outside the United States because it is less expensive for them. Yes, the bottom line. Lobster is the most financially lucrative product in Maine, but there are worries that global warming may have a harmful effect in the future. Lobster is closely connected to our tourism industry and is vital to the economy of the Downeast area.

Researchers and scientists are trying to figure out ways to repair mistakes of the past that have affected fish and foods and look toward the future to make our foods safe and plentiful. Studies of the migration of fish and lobster because of global warming are much easier to see and understand through the internet. Lobster and tourism are extremely important in Maine and particularly in Downeast Maine. Maine has a good system for regulating the catch of lobster. We are in a good place today and filling the current demand, but we also look at what is happening to the waters warming in the Bay of Maine. The shortage of some fish in southern New England as the fish and lobster migrate to colder waters have Downeast fishermen looking back over their shoulders and worried that someday they will haul in their traps and they will be empty.

Beech Hill Farm. *Courtesy of the College of the Atlantic.*

In fifty years, could lobster go the way of our shrimp industry? We are learning fast, and that should bring some of the answers and solutions we hope for.

Downeast has always been somewhat self-sufficient. Experience in living has taught residents that. Organic gardens and having a small garden space are natural here.

We are learning more about ingredients online and easily find facts about nutrients in food as well as the additives that are put in our food today. The products you want and are not in your grocery store are available online. As an overmedicated and overweight society, there can be awareness of what we are doing to ourselves and an open mind to learning more. Organic foods are an important factor in taking care of your body. Today, you may think you are doing well by eating apples, spinach, grapes, peaches and so forth, but if you don't use organic foods, you should understand that spinach, as well as many other fruits and vegetables, is heavily sprayed by pesticides.

We are able to travel and prepare diverse menus. How will this affect the foods that our future generations eat? Perhaps they may create a whole new type of food we have never heard of or even thought about.

The Jackson Laboratories is a worldwide research center based in Bar Harbor, Maine. The labs are making advancements in the study of cancer, Alzheimer's disease, heart ailments and many other diseases that affect people.

In an interview with Edwin Liu, CEO/president of Jackson Labs, he suggested that a person's diet should be for the individual. I was hoping for that magic food that I could slip into my diet, but something he said has stayed with me. It was his comment about a dog's food. He mentioned how dog food manufacturers are going back to meat for dogs and not foods that are foreign to the ancestry of what dogs ate. He said people are different. There is no perfect diet that would fit all humans. People have different DNA and backgrounds. Exercise should be for what an individual is able to do and then do it on a consistent basis. He does suggest that health studies reinforce the idea that everyone should include exercise, have a balanced diet, moderation of calories and no smoking. He said he didn't include moderate drinking, as it is subjective as to what is moderate.

Liu was born in China, and he feels that Chinese people really don't eat as many vegetables as we might think and their diets have sauces and fats that create health issues too. American advertising, he said, stresses an importance on large portions and food that is a bargain. Three problems for health that he recognizes are smoking, sun and pesticides.

Researchers such as Gareth Howell at Jackson are finding wonderful discoveries about vitamins in foods that will help repair our bodies and may keep us from developing certain diseases. It is exciting to think that it may be possible to control glaucoma in the future by having enough of a certain part of niacin (B3). Some foods that are rich in vitamin B3 are turkey, chicken, peanuts, mushrooms and tuna.

Niacin-rich meals that sound pretty good include this easy dinner:

Chicken Breast with Lightly Sautéed Mushrooms and Crispy Sage

Chicken breast
Olive oil
Sage
½ to 1 cup mushrooms

Broil chicken, and while that is cooking, add a few tablespoons of olive oil to a pan and quickly cook sage until crispy, then take it from the pan. Sauté mushrooms in same oil and pour over chicken. Sprinkle sage on top.

THE JESSUP LIBRARY IN Bar Harbor has a book sale each summer. I noticed an article on the cover of *Science News Magazine* from March 19, 2016, titled "The Beauty of FAT." It just may be the ultimate body repair kit. It sounded like something enjoyable to read.

From the article "Fat Is a Fixer," by Susan Gaidos:

> *Most people would be happy to get rid of excess body fat. Even better: Trade the spare tire for something useful—say, better-functioning knees or hips, or a fix for an ailing heart or a broken bone. The idea is not far-fetched, some scientists say. Researchers worldwide are repurposing discarded fat to repair body parts damaged by injury, disease or age. Recent studies in lab animals and humans show that the much-maligned material can be a source of cells useful for treating a wide range of ills.*
>
> *Plastic Surgeon J. Peter Rubin, also at Pitt, says that the multitalented cells found in fat could prove to be the ultimate body repair kit, providing replacement tissue or inspiring repair of body parts that can't mend themselves.*

According to the article, fat cells aren't all bad. They are the body's repair kit, and they pack up and go to try to repair injuries or disease. My wording, not theirs, but doesn't that make you feel good?

THE INTERNET HAS INTRODUCED food information that is overwhelming. Availability of foods from all over the world results in an exploration for new tastes. Still, there is the yearning for a connection to past memories of simple comfort food.

There are thoughtful people who live here and people who come to visit here. There is a fellow who wants no credit for a pretty unique and

Baking cookies and giving them to friends in honor of relatives who have died. *Author's collection.*

thoughtful endeavor that he does regularly. He has fond memories of his grandmother's cookies. What could be nicer than a person honoring his grandmother who was born in the late 1800s and honoring his mother by baking his grandmother's cookies and giving them away free with her recipe. These are a nice soft molasses cookie and a good way to pause, have a cookie and a cup of tea and appreciate "life the way it should be."

Grandma Clara Clement's Gingersnap Cookies

2 cups unsalted butter, soft, melted
2 cups sugar
2 eggs
8 tablespoons molasses
5 cups all-purpose flour
4 teaspoons baking soda
4 teaspoons ground ginger
4 teaspoons ground cinnamon
2 teaspoons group cloves

Cream butter and sugar well. Add eggs and molasses and mix well. Mix in dry ingredients. Chill well, covered (overnight or until cookie dough is cold and firm).

Roll into balls (about the size of large walnuts), then roll in sugar and place on a non-stick cookie sheet at least 2 inches apart.

Bake about 15 minutes at 350 degrees in a preheated oven until cookies are cracked and lightly brown. Enjoy!

*Note that the recipe didn't say that the balls should be flattened, and larger cookies work well also.

SOURCES

Abbe Museum, Bar Harbor, Maine

Barbara and Dick Fox, Bar Harbor, Maine

Bar Harbor Historical Society, Bar Harbor, Maine

Bouchard, Kelley. "Portland Rum Riot." *Portland Herald*, October 2, 2011.

Burrage, Henry D.D. *The Beginning of Colonial Maine, 1602–1658.* Portland, ME: Marks Printing House, 1914.

Catherine Lambrecht, Chicago Culinary Historians, Greater Midwest Foodways Alliance, Chicago, Illinois

Charlene and Jeremy Cates, lobstermen, Cutler, Maine

Colonies, Ships, and Pirates: Concerning History in the Atlantic World, 1680–1740. Csphistorical.com.

Cooking for Henry, Chef Jan Willemsen, Ford Research Institute

Coolidge, A.J. *A History and Description of New England, General and Local.* Vol. 1, *Maine, New Hampshire, and Vermont.* Boston: A.J. Coolidge, 1859.

Dixon, Roland Burrage. *The Early Migration of the Indians of New England and the Maritime Provinces.* Worcester, MA: American Antiquarian Society, 1914.

Dubin, Arthur. *Some Classic Trains.* Milwaukee, WI: Kalmbach Publishing, 1969.

Fishermen's Voice 23, no. 8 (August 2018).

Ford Research Institute

40 Hayseeders

Hancock Historical Society

Jessup Memorial Library, Bar Harbor, Maine

Kilby, William Henry. *Eastport and Passamaquoddy: A Collection of Historial and Biological Sketches*. Eastport, ME: E.E. Shead, 1888.

Kolinsky, Mark. *Cod: A Biography of the Fish that Changed the World*. New York: Penguin Books, 1998.

Languages of the Americas: Native American Culture, native-languages.org.

Maine Research Institute

Marilyn Granzyk, Chicago, Illinois

Mount Desert Island Historical Society, Mount Desert, Maine

Muriel Davisson, Tremont, Maine

Nearing, Helen. *Loving and Leaving the Good Life*. Post Mills, VT: Chelsea Green Publishing, 1992.

Newberry Library, Edward Curtis Letters, Chicago, Illinois

New England Historical Society

Prins, Harald E.L., and Bunny McBride. "Asticou's Island Domain: Wabanaki Peoples at Mount Desert Island 1500–2000." Acadia National Park Ethnographic Overview and Assessment. Vol. 2. Boston: National Park Service, 2007.

Ralph Stanley, talks given at Southwest Harbor Library, Southwest Harbor, Maine.

Ruggles House Historical Home Museum, Columbia Falls, Maine

Seal Cove Auto Museum, Seal Cove, Maine

Smithsonian.com.

Stephanie Clement, Bar Harbor, Maine

Street, George E. *Mount Desert: A History*. Edited by Samuel A. Eliot. N.p., 1926.

Tremont Historical Society, Bass Harbor, Maine

Verrill, A. Hyatt. *Foods America Gave the World*. Boston: L.C. Page and Company, 1937.

Williamson, William D. *The History of the State of Maine*. Hallowell, ME: Glazier, Masters, 1832.

Woodard, Colin. *The Lobster Coast*. New York: Penguin Books, 2004.